WATER INTO WINE AND THE BEHEADING OF JOHN THE BAPTIST

Number 150
WATER INTO WINE AND THE
BEHEADING OF JOHN THE BAPTIST

by
Roger Aus

WATER INTO WINE AND THE
BEHEADING OF JOHN THE BAPTIST
Early Jewish-Christian Interpretation of
Esther 1 in John 2:1-11 and Mark 6:17-29

by
Roger Aus

Scholars Press
Atlanta, Georgia

WATER INTO WINE AND THE
BEHEADING OF JOHN THE BAPTIST
Early Jewish-Christian Interpretation of
Esther 1 in John 2:1-11 and Mark 6:17-29

© 1988
Brown University

Library of Congress Cataloging in Publication Data

Aus, Roger, 1940-
    Water into wine and the beheading of John the
Baptist.
    (Brown Judaic studies ; no. 150)
    Includes index.
    I. Bible. O.T. Esther I--Criticism, interpretation,
etc. 2. Bible. N.T. John II, 1-11--Criticism,
interpretation, etc. 3. Bible. N.T. Mark VI, 17-29--
Criticism, interpretation, etc. I. Title. II. Series.
BS1375.2.A97   1988   222'.906   88-11521
ISBN 1-55540-245-3

Printed in the United States of America
on acid-free paper

To

Dagny Brevig Aus

an understanding and generous mother

Contents

Preface

The first Christians were all Jews. In interpreting the significance of Jesus to their coreligionists and others, they naturally employed primarily those materials and methods known from their own use of the Hebrew Bible at home, in the synagogue, and the rabbinic academies. In addition to halakhic or legal matters, there was already much in Scripture of a narrative, descriptive nature. It easily lent itself to further interpretation, just as Chronicles commented on and modified Kings. This *haggadah* / *'agadah* became very popular, filling out details missing in the text and expanding upon certain features, especially in regard to Israel's great heroes and opponents.

In regard to the latter, it is significant that Louis Ginzberg's monumental study *The Legends of the Jews* begins with the creation, but ceases with Esther. This biblical book describes not only the origins of the Purim festival, but also the greatest testing of Judaism since the slavery of the Israelites in Egypt – the threat of total annihilation. It is no wonder the narrative became so popular, and that haggadic embellishment of it spread so quickly.

Two extensive accounts in the gospels of the "New" Testament reflect a major knowledge and appropriation of the Esther story, especially its first chapter: Jesus' transformation of water into wine in John 2, and the beheading of John the Baptist in Mark 6. They clearly show the same type of retelling and reforming/adapting a biblical story found elsewhere in haggadic accounts, and they attest the very creative abilities of first-century Jewish Christians. As I note in the text, however, the historical categories of "true" and "false" are simply inappropriate in regard to this type of material. Conservative Christians (and Orthodox Jews) I invite to consider the *religious truths* behind these and similar narratives.

My sincere thanks go to Dr. Niko Oswald of Berlin, and Rabbi Joseph Asher of San Francisco, for helping me to vocalize Hebrew and Aramaic phrases[1], and to the Rev. Philip Quanbeck of Minneapolis, and Professor Étan Levine of Haifa, for reading the essay on Mark 6. I am also grateful to The Max Richter Foundation of Rhode Island for subsidizing the costs involved in printing this volume. Finally, Jacob Neusner, who through his manifold translations of rabbinical works and his methodological studies has opened up

---

[1]In the text, the letter ח is represented by "ch," as in German "Bach."

the field of Judaica to completely new audiences, very generously accepted the volume for this series. To him and my other Jewish friends in the United States, Israel, and Germany I can only express my humble thanks for being allowed to share in the richness of the cultivated olive tree (Rom 11:17).

Roger David Aus

July, 1987
West Berlin, Germany

Part One

THE WEDDING FEAST AT CANA (JOHN 2:1-11), AND AHASUERUS' WEDDING FEAST IN JUDAIC TRADITIONS ON ESTHER 1

One NT scholar writing recently on miracles labels the wedding feast at Cana an "enigmatic account."[1] Because Jesus' transformation of water into wine at Cana is the Evangelist's leadoff miracle, he obviously attaches great importance to it. Yet it is indeed enigmatic. The present-day reader asks questions like the following. If according to John 6:42 Joseph is still alive, why is "the mother of Jesus" at the wedding in 2:1 without her husband? In v. 12 Jesus' brothers accompany him from Cana to Capernaum. Why then are they invisible in vv. 1-11? Was the wine's giving out only due to poor planning? What kind of attitude towards Jesus lies behind Mary's simple statement to him: "They have no wine"? What authority does she have to command the servants of other people? Why is there no public reaction to the miracle, called a "sign" here?

At least several of these questions can be resolved if one considers that the author has here very creatively adapted for his own purposes Judaic haggadic traditions on the feast(s) of Ahasuerus in Esther 1:1-8.[2] Before analyzing the various elements of that adaptation in Section III, however, it will first be helpful to view the Scroll of Esther and "signs" in Jewish tradition (Section I), and to recognize the Persian setting and mood of Esther 1:1-8 (Section II).

---

[1]H.C. Kee, *Miracle in the Early Christian World.* A Study in Socio-historical Method (New Haven: Yale, 1983) 230.
[2]The Evangelist most probably found most of 2:1-11 already in a source. On the so-called "signs source," see Section V, B.

I. THE BOOK OF ESTHER AND SIGNS/MIRACLES

The Book or Scroll of Esther in its first Hebrew form may go back to the fourth century B.C.E. The final form definitely emerged by the second century B.C.E.[3] The festival of Purim described in ch. 9, to be kept "year by year," is mentioned by Josephus at the end of the first century C.E.,[4] and was certainly already observed by Palestinian Jews in the first half of that century. Part of the observance of this annual festival was the obligatory reading of the entire Scroll of Esther in Hebrew, in the synagogue, by all Aramaic-speaking adult males.[5] That many had even memorized it is shown in m. Meg. 2:1, which states that one does not fulfill one's obligation if one only reads it by heart.[6] In t. Meg. 2:5, an incident is related of R. Meir's not finding a Scroll of Esther in a town he visits. Thus he simply writes one out from memory and reads from it.[7]

Why was this biblical book so popular?[8] The main reason was not the merriment, including drinking, encouraged at the festival of Purim,[9] but what Josephus mentions at the very outset of his retelling of the Esther narrative: "the entire nation of the Jews, with their wives and children, was in danger of

---

[3]C.A. Moore, *Esther* (AB 7B; Garden City, New York: Doubleday, 1979) LVII - LX.

[4]*Ant.* 11.295 (6.13). For Josephus I employ the LCL edition, here in the translation of R. Marcus. See 2 Macc 15:36 for "Mordecai's day," the fourteenth of Adar.

[5]See t. Meg. 2:1-9 in J. Neusner, *The Tosefta* (New York: KTAV, 1981) 2.284-86. Cf. the opinion of R. Meir, a third generation Tanna (see H. Strack and G. Stemberger, *Einleitung in Talmud und Midrasch* [Munich: Beck, 1982] 82), in m. Meg. 2:3, in H. Danby, The *Mishnah* (Oxford: Oxford University, 1964) 203. In y. Meg. 2:4 (French in M. Schwab, *Le Talmud de Jerusalem* [Paris: Maisonneuve, 1960] 4.231-32), Rab says Meir's opinion was adopted as the general rule. Bar Qappara, a fifth generation Tanna (Strack and Stemberger, *Einleitung* 88), states in y. Meg. 2:5(4) (Schwab 4.233) that one is also required to recite the Esther narrative before women and children. That is, the reading also belonged in the home, and not only in the synagogue. All partook in the festival.

[6]Danby, *The Mishnah* 203.

[7]Neusner, *The Tosefta* 2.284-85. In y. Meg. 4:1 (Schwab 4.246) this incident is referred to, and other examples are given of rabbis who can write out "all texts by heart."

[8]Moore, *Esther* LVII, points out in regard to Esther's popularity the large number of midrashim on this book. They are enumerated in L.B. Paton, *The Book of Esther* (ICC; Edinburgh: Clark, 1908) 101-03; see also the art. "Esther" by E. Hirsch in *J.E.* (1904) 5.234. Moore also notes that of the prophets and the hagiographa, only Esther has two targums. In y. Meg. 1:5(4),70d (Schwab 4.207) it is stated that even if the prophets and the hagiographa would one day become invalid, the festival of Esther (Purim) and its legal regulations would not cease.

[9]In b. Meg. 7b (Soncino English translation by M. Simon, 38), Raba, a fourth generation Babylonian Amora (Strack and Stemberger, *Einleitung* 99), states: "It is the duty of a man to mellow himself (with wine) on Purim until he cannot tell the difference between 'cursed be Haman' and 'blessed be Mordecai.'"

being destroyed" (Esther 3:13, through Haman); yet Ahasuerus' second queen, the successor of Vashti, "saved our nation."[10] Not since Pharaoh's decree to cast all male Hebrew children into the Nile (Exod 1:22) had such a danger threatened the entire Jewish people.[11]

This deliverance from Haman's plotting was considered a miracle in Jewish sources. For no other biblical book is the term "sign" (Hebrew נֵס, Aramaic נִיסָא), in the sense of "miracle," employed so often in rabbinic literature. In the running commentary on Esther found in b. Meg. 10b - 17a,[12] it occurs at 13b, 14a, and 15b, as well as in 2b, 3b, 4a, and 19a (twice).[13] It is also found in 1 Targ. Est. 9:26 and 29,[14] and in 2 Targ. Est. 2:6,11; 4:13; 6:11; 7:10; 9:26 and 29.[15] The statement found in b. Ber. 57b is typical: "our rabbis taught" that "one who sees the Scroll of Esther (in a dream) will have a miracle wrought for him."[16]

It is also important to note that R. Assi, either a first- or third-generation Amora,[17] could state that "just as the dawn is the end of the whole night, so is the story of Esther the end of all the miracles" (סוֹף כָּל הַנִּסִּים).[18] In the official chronology of early Judaism, Seder 'Olam, it is also stated in chapter 21 regarding Esther 9:29 that Esther is the sixth and last of the scriptural prophetesses.[19] If, as seems probable, this was also maintained by Palestinian Jews in the first century C.E., the author of John 2:1-11 probably intentionally implies a connection between Jesus' first "sign" (v. 11) and the last "sign" found

---

[10]*Ant.* 11.184-85 (6.1). Cf. 2 Bar. 68.
[11]See Midr. Ps. 22/6 on Ps 22:2, as well as 22/15 on Ps 22:1. English in W. Braude, *The Midrash on Psalms* (New Haven: Yale, 1959) 1.303 and 309-10, respectively.
[12]Soncino English 56-102.
[13]Soncino English 78, 81, 92, 7, 14, 15, and 117, respectively.
[14]See B. Grossfeld, *The First Targum to Esther* (New York: Sepher-Hermon, 1983) 35 and 71, and 36 and 72.
[15]I employ the edition of P. Cassel in his *Aus Literatur und Geschichte. Zweites Targum zum Buche Esther. Im vocalisirten Urtext* (Leipzig and Berlin: Friedrich, 1885). An English translation of this work is included in his *An Explanatory Commentary on Esther*, trans. A. Bernstein (Edinburgh: Clark, 1888) 263-344. I thank W. Meeks of Yale for making the latter available to me. Another translation available to me is that of A. Sulzbach, *Targum Scheni zum Buch Esther* (Frankfurt am Main: Kauffmann, 1920). The Midrash on Psalm 22, interpreted by the rabbis in light of the Scroll of Esther, also notes miracles at 22/16 on Ps 22:1; 22/26 on Ps 22:17; and 22/27 on Ps 22:20 (see Braude 1.311, 320 and 321 respectively).
[16]Soncino 355-56.
[17]Strack and Stemberger, *Einleitung* 91 and 94.
[18]See b. Yoma 29a (Soncino 136), noted by P. Billerbeck in *Str-B* 2.410. A parallel is found in Midr. Ps. 22/10 on Ps 22:1 (Braude 1.306).
[19]I employ the edition of C. Milikowsky, *Seder Olam: A Rabbinic Chronography* (1981 Yale Ph.D. dissertation) 356 and 510.

in Scripture. Jesus' first miracle is even greater than the last miracle of the Hebrew Bible.

Finally, m. Mid. 1:3 relates that there were five gates to the Herodian Temple in Jerusalem. Above the Eastern Gate there was a "representation of the palace of Susa."[20] In b. Menach. 98a one rabbi explains the reason for this: "So that they be ever mindful whence they came."[21] The English translator in the Soncino edition of this passage, E. Cashdan, in turn comments in his n. 1 on the foregoing statement: "From the exile in Persia, and so would offer thanks to God at all times for their deliverance."

Although the archaeology of Herod's Temple is a much debated question, I find it hard to believe that the Mishnah in two separate tractates would mention something that never existed.[22] If the palace of Susa was depicted above the Eastern Gate of the Temple, not only Jerusalemites, but also those Jews who came from all other parts of Palestine and from the diaspora for the annual pilgrimage festivals, would have been reminded in a concrete way not only of the return of the Jews from the Babylonian Captivity through the Persian Cyrus, but also of God's delivering them there through Esther from Haman's plan of total destruction. The palace of Susa in Persia, the setting of Ahasuerus' wedding feast(s) in Judaic traditions on Esther 1, was thus probably also known visually to most Palestinians and some diaspora Jews in the first half of the first century C.E.

II. THE PERSIAN SETTING OF ESTHER 1

Modern commentators agree that Ahasuerus is the Achaemenian king Xerxes I, who reigned from 486 – 465 B.C.E., and was the son of Darius I.[23] The latter came to Susa, the earlier Elamite capital, from the region of Persia, as Herodotus, writing in the fifth century B.C.E., notes in 3.70.[24] Although

---

[20]Danby 590. Cf. Kelim 17:9 (Danby 629).
[21]Soncino 599. R. Chisda and R. Isaac b. Abdimi, the speakers here, were both third generation Babylonian Amoraim. Cf. Strack and Stemberger, *Einleitung* 96.
[22]M. Avi-Yonah, art. "Shushan" in *E.J.* (1971) 14. 1484, accepts the representation of Susa on the East Gate. This is also the opinion of M. Simon, the Soncino English translator of Middot ("Introduction"). T. Busink, *Der Tempel von Jerusalem von Salomo bis Herodes* (Leiden: Brill, 1980) 2.1542, considers Middot merely a plan for the future.
[23]Cf. the convenient table in Moore, *Esther* 116, as well as XXXV. See also G. Gerleman, *Esther* (BKAT 21; Neukirchen-Vluyn: Neukirchener, 1973) 50-51. After the first Addition, the LXX at Esther 1:1 falsely reads Artaxerxes; it is followed by Josephus in *Ant.* 11.184.
[24]For the dating, see the LCL translation by A.D. Godley in 1.vii. A.T. Olmstead in his *History of the Persian Empire (Achaemenid Period)* (Chicago: University of Chicago, 1948) 167 falsely refers to 3.129. Darius' accession to the throne is mentioned in Dan 5:31, a chapter very important in regard to the motif of "being changed." See Section III, J.

Ahasuerus' later capital Persepolis far surpassed his first residence, the citadel at Susa was itself "unusually beautiful," as Darius himself states on the base of a column there.[25] In a record preserved in a foundation box, the same king notes that the "splendid work" included cedar timber from Lebanon and teakwood; lapis lazuli, carnelian and turquoise stones; silver, copper, ivory, stone pillars, gold, inlays, adorned baked brick, and adorned walls.[26] There were paved courts, a harem, a throne-room over 192 feet (58.5 meters) square, a paradise or garden, and a treasury.[27] This physical description of the palace is in part reflected in Esther 1:2, 5-6.

The treasury at Susa was full of gold and silver objects, for Darius obtained tribute from as far away as Ethiopia. Most of the gold, however, came from India. The combined total of all annual tribute in the form of gold and silver according to Herodotus was 14,560 talents.[28] The countries just mentioned correspond to the India and Ethiopia mentioned in Esther 1:1. Because of them, Ahasuerus was considered by the rabbis to rule over the whole world, like Solomon.[29] For this reason 2 Targ. Est. 1:1 lists him as the sixth of the ten kings who once ruled or will rule the whole world, the ninth being the King Messiah, the son of David, and the tenth God.[30]

Writing in the first century B.C.E., Strabo notes in his *Geography* that in Susa "each of the kings built for himself a separate habitation, treasure-houses *(thēsaurous),* and storage-places for what tributes they each exacted, as memorials of his administration."[31]

Ahasuerus had already inherited all the wealth mentioned above from his father Darius, and the tribute kept on flowing in during his own reign in addition. It is no wonder there is a rabbinic tradition on Dan 11:2 asserting that

---

[25]See Olmstead, *History* 171.

[26]*Ibid.,* 168, with the sources of the inscription in n.17. Plate LVI is an illustration of winged bulls on glazed bricks, attesting Darius' description. See also the color plates of two archers, a lion griffin, a winged bull, and a lion from fifth century B.C.E. Susa in R. Ghirshman, *Iran,* ed. A. Malraux and G. Salles, trans. E. Edzard ("Universum der Kunst"; Munich: Beck, 1964) 141-43. An English translation, not available to me, is noted in Moore, *Esther* LXVII–LXVIII.

[27]Olmstead, *History* 168-70. An aerial photo of the palace and a plan of it are found in Ghirshman, *Iran* 138-39.

[28]See 3.94-96.

[29]See the Addition at LXX Esther 1:13; b. Meg. 11a (Soncino 63); Esther Rab. 1/4 on Esther 1:1 (Soncino 9.21); 2 Targ. Esther 1:1 (Cassel, *Commentary* 267); and other sources cited in L. Ginzberg, *The Legends of the Jews* (Philadelphia: Jewish Publication Society of America, 1968) 6.457, n.47.

[30]See Cassel, *Commentary* 263. In the Esther Rabbah passage mentioned in n.29, the Messiah also occurs.

[31]Translation by H.L. Jones in the LCL edition of XV.3.21, where Strabo says he relies on "Polycritus." For Strabo as born in 64 or 63 B.C.E., see 1.xiv.

Ahasuerus is the fourth Persian king "far richer" than his predecessors.[32] When he is described in Esther 1:4 as showing the "riches of his royal glory and the splendor and pomp of his majesty" (RSV) for all of 180 days at his banquet, the early Jewish reader aware of the Persian kings' wealth would not react to this statement as skeptically as we do today.

Two elements certainly aided in communicating knowledge of Persian conditions to the Jews. First, a considerable number of the latter still lived in Babylonia (then Parthia) in the first century C.E.[33] Secondly, Aramaic was the *lingua franca* of the Persians.[34] Aramaic-speaking Jews thus had easy access to Persian narratives.

One final aspect of Persian behavior and wealth must be mentioned here, the relevance of which to John 2:1-11 I shall presently show. Herodotus writes in 1.133 regarding the Persians that "they are greatly given to wine" at their feasts. In 1.212, for example, the queen of the Massagatae, Tomyris, says to Cyrus regarding wine: "the fruit of the vine – that fruit whereof you Persians drink even to madness."[35] Xenophon even maintains that the successors of Cyrus eat and drink all day, drinking so much that "they are themselves carried out when they are no longer able to stand straight enough to walk out."[36] R. Joseph (ben Chiyya), a third generation Babylonian Amora,[37] mirrors this sentiment when he says the Persians "eat and drink like bears."[38]

At their feasts they employed beautiful couches and exquisitely fashioned drinking vessels of gold. Strabo writes in his *Geography* XV 3:19: "Persians dine in an extravagant manner, serving whole animals in great numbers and of various kinds; and their couches, as also their drinking-cups *(ekpōmata)* and everything else, are so brilliantly ornamented that they gleam with silver and gold." Herodotus in 7.119 notes that while campaigning with his army, Xerxes made his host town provide him with "gold and silver cups and bowls *(potēria te*

---

[32]See Pirq. R. El. 49. English in G. Friedlander, *Pirke de Rabbi Eliezer* (New York: Hermon, 1970; original London, 1916) 392. Probably because of Ahasuerus' futile campaign to conquer all of Greece, he was thought to fulfill Dan 11:2b.

[33]See G. Stemberger, *Das klassische Judentum* (Munich: Beck, 1979) 39-40.

[34]See Olmstead, *History* 245, as well as J. Naveh and J. Greenfield, "Hebrew and Aramaic in the Persian Period," in *The Cambridge History of Judaism,* ed. W.D. Davies and L. Finkelstein, I. Introduction, The Persian Period (Cambridge: Cambridge University, 1984) 116 and 119.

[35]See also 5.18 ("flushed as they were with excess of wine") and 19 ("you are...truly drunk").

[36]*Cyropaedia* VIII.8.9-10 in the LCL translation of W. Miller. In 8.7 Xenophon says the Persians "take great pride also in having as many drinking-cups *(ekpōmata)* as possible." The section may be an early insertion.

[37]Strack and Stemberger, *Einleitung* 97.

[38]In b. Meg. 11a (Soncino 60), commenting on Dan 7:5. Parallels are found in b. Abodah Zarah 2b (Soncino 3) and b. Qid. 72a (Soncino 368).

kai krētēras) and all manner of service for the table."[39]   At Pausanias' defeat of the Persians, the Greeks found in the camp of Xerxes "couches gilded and silver-plated, and golden bowls and cups and other drinking-vessels" *(krētēras te chryseous kai phialas te kai alla ekpōmata).*[40]   These rough, battlefield conditions help to convey how much more luxurious Ahasuerus' palace feast at home in Susa must have been with its "couches of gold and silver" and "golden goblets" (Esther 1:6-7).

Archaeological finds in Persia/Iran convey the same impression of extreme luxury already gained. An exquisitely fashioned fifth century B.C.E. golden bowl with the name Xerxes, from Teheran, is pictured in Ghirshman, as is a golden drinking cup designed as the rear of a beautiful winged lion, from the same city.[41]   In his commentary on Esther, Moore pictures a somewhat shorter cup from the Metropolitan Museum in New York City.[42]

All of the above information provides the setting and the mood[43] for Jewish interpretation of the feast(s) of Ahasuerus in Esther 1. They, in turn, provide the major background of Jesus' miracle at Cana, which W. Bauer aptly called a "luxury miracle."[44]

III. JESUS AND WEDDING IMAGERY, AND JUDAIC INTERPRETATIONS OF ESTHER 1:1-8 AS THE BACKGROUND OF JESUS' SIGN IN JOHN 2:1-11

In the following, section A describes Jesus' association with a wedding and wine elsewhere in the NT; section B links the days of the Messiah to a wedding; and section C shows how Ahasuerus' (wedding) feast was compared to the messianic banquet in rabbinic tradition. The eight sections D to K then examine the dependence of John 2:1-11 on Judaic interpretations of Esther 1.

A. Jesus, a Wedding, and Wine

In John 3:29 John the Baptist labels himself the friend of the bridegroom, the latter being Jesus. According to the Synoptics, Jesus compared himself to a bridegroom. When people asked him why his disciples did not fast, while those of John the Baptist and the Pharisees did, he replied: "Can the wedding guests fast while the bridegroom is with them?" Then he contrasted new wine and old wineskins (Mark 2:18-22 par.). This association of Jesus, a wedding (at which

---

[39]See 7.190.

[40]Herodotus 9.80.

[41]See *Iran* 256 and 242, respectively.

[42]*Esther,* between pp. 22-23. It is also found in his *Studies in the Book of Esther* (New York: KTAV, 1982) 376.

[43]The "Persian mood" of Esther 1 is enhanced by the fact that six of the ten Persian nouns in Esther are found there. See Moore, *Esther* XLI.

[44]*Das Johannesevangelium* (HNT 6; Tübingen: Mohr, 1933³) 46.

no fasting was allowed), and wine may have been known to the author of John 2:1-11. If so, it encouraged him to create a narrative with a marriage feast and wine, and with Jesus as the central figure.

B. A Wedding and the Days of the Messiah

In early Judaism the days of the Messiah were compared to a wedding. Yalqut Shim'oni on Cant 3:11 § 988 states, for example: "'On the day of his wedding': These are the days of the Messiah, for the Holy One, blessed be He, is compared to a bridegroom, (as it is written): 'as the bridegroom rejoices over the bride, (so shall your God rejoice over you)' (Isa 62:5)."[45] Other sources substantiate this.[46]

In light of this, as well as A., Jesus' activity at the Cana wedding can be described as having messianic undertones. The early Jewish reader asked: Have the days of the Messiah begun to come through the ministry of Jesus?

C. Ahasuerus' (Wedding) Feast and the Messianic Banquet

Ahasuerus' banquet lasted 180 days (Esther 1:3-4). Regarding this, Est. Rab. 2/4 relates that R. Chiyya, a fifth generation Tanna,[47] had a (non-Jewish) friend who served him a banquet with all that was created during the six days of creation. He then asked Chiyya: "What can your God do for you (at the Messianic banquet, the feast of Leviathan) more than this?" He replied: "Your repast has a limit, but the repast which our God will provide for the righteous in the time to come will have no limit," as Isa 64:3 is interpreted.[48] According to Est. Rab. 2/5 on Esther 1:5, Ahasuerus himself asks the Jews participating in his magnificent feast: "Can your God do more for you than this?" They also answer with Isa 64:3, adding: "If He provides for us nothing better than this feast (in the time to come), we could say to Him, 'We have already enjoyed the like of this at the table of Ahasuerus.'"[49]

Ahasuerus' banquet in Esther 1:3-4 is thus associated in Judaic tradition with the messianic banquet, at which excellent, old wine is to be served.[50] Since

---

[45] I owe this reference to P. Cassel, *Die Hochzeit von Cana theologisch und historisch in Symbol, Kunst und Legende ausgelegt* (Berlin: Schulze, 1883) 69.

[46] Cf. Exod. Rab. Bo 15/30 on Exod 12:2 (Soncino 3.204), as well as other passages cited in *Str-B* 1.517-18.

[47] Strack and Stemberger, *Einleitung* 87.

[48] Soncino 9.36.

[49] Soncino 9.38. On the messianic banquet, see the many sources cited in *Str-B* 4.1154-65, including parallels to this passage on p. 1156.

[50] See, for example, Targ. Cant 8:2, which has the Messiah, the feast of Leviathan, and the drinking of old wine (*Str-B* 4.1148). For the wine preserved for the righteous since the six days of creation, see Ginzberg, *Legends* 1.19-20 and notes. See also Pesiq. R. 37, where God will make for the Messiah seven canopies of precious stones and pearls. Out of each canopy will flow four rivers,

John 2:1-11 is for the most part based on motifs from Ahasuerus' banquet (see sections D-K), the issue must be raised of whether Jesus' first sign is not intended to point to the messianic banquet. The expected great quantity and quality of wine are already present at the wedding feast of Cana through Jesus' sign. They thus point to the messianic days as present, and to Jesus as the Messiah.

D. Ahasuerus' Wedding Feast

John 2:1-11 describes a wedding feast. The term "wedding" is mentioned in both vv. 1 and 2, "bridegroom" in v. 9, the "steward of the feast" (RSV) in vv. 8-9, servants in vv. 5 and 9, and "wine," a basic element in a wedding feast, in vv. 3, 9-10.

Already in the LXX, the feast (מִשְׁתֶּה) which Ahasuerus makes in Esther 1:3 is also interpreted in v. 5 as: "When the days of the marriage *(tou gamou)* were completed." That is, this banquet lasting 180 days was his and Vashti's wedding feast. This is not a scribal error, as suggested by Moore,[51] for the early Jewish translators understood the מִשְׁתֶּה of v. 3 in its later sense of "wedding feast."[52] Other passages in the LXX of Esther corroborate this. At 2:18, instead of "Then the king gave a great banquet to all his princes and servants; it was Esther's banquet," it reads: "And the king made a banquet for all his friends and magnates for seven days, and he made a great ceremony of (lit., 'exalted') the marriage to Esther." Thus he treated his first and second queens equally, with lavish wedding feasts.[53] In Esther 9:22 the annual festival of Purim, described in the MT as "days of feasting," is also changed by the LXX into "good days of marriages and rejoicing." Finally, three midrashim on Esther also consider Ahasuerus' banquet of Esther 1:3 as his marriage feast with Vashti.[54]

John 2:1-11 and Esther 1 in Judaic tradition thus both describe wedding feasts.

---

one of them consisting of wine. English in W. Braude, *Pesikta Rabbati* (New Haven: Yale, 1968) 687.

[51]*Esther* 40.

[52]Cf. M. Jastrow, *A Dictionary of the Targumim, the Talmud Babli and Yerushalmi, and the Midrashic Literature* (New York: Pardes, 1950) 859 for the Hebrew and Aramaic. "House of the feast" means, for example, "wedding house."

[53]The so-called "Lucianic" text at 2:18 also has: "And the king married Esther in all splendour." It is a Greek translation independent of the LXX. See now D. Clines, *The Esther Scroll: The Story of the Story* (JSOT Supplement Series 30; Sheffield: JSOT, 1984) 72 and 93. He has printed the text and translated it; 2:18 is on p. 223.

[54]Cf. Ginzberg, *Legends* 6.452, n.6. At many points, the Second Targum is so expansive that it can also be called a midrash.

E. Good Wine at the End, and Lack of Wine

In John 2:10 the steward of the marriage feast tells the bridegroom after Jesus' changing the water into wine: "Every man serves the good wine first; and when men have drunk freely, then the poor wine; but you have kept the good wine until now."   P. Cassel calls this remark "der frivole Witz des Speisemeisters,"[55] and C.H. Dodd notes here a "touch of homely humour."[56] Up to now no real parallel from classical or Judaic sources has been found.[57] This statement, however, derives from Judaic haggada on Ahasuerus' marriage banquet.

Esther 1:4 states that the (marriage) banquet mentioned in v. 3 lasted "for many days, 180 days." Est. Rab. 2/3 and 4 on this verse relate three narratives, one beginning and two ending with the phrase, "The last day was as good as the first": יוֹם אַחֲרוֹן כְּיוֹם רִשׁוֹן.[58]

The second narrative deals with Bar Lufyeni from Sepphoris, who gave his daughter in marriage to a man in Acco, some thirty miles (fifty kilometers) distant. The father was so wealthy that he set up booths in which wine was served on the entire route, and

> gold lamps were strung from one place to the other. It is reported that before they had finished he was giving them beans from the threshing floor to eat and (new, poor) wine from the vat to drink. R. Abun said: "And what is more, it was served in smoke-stained jars." Here, however, (in the feast of Ahasuerus), the last day was as good as the first.[59]

In this narrative poor calculation causes the good wine to go out at a marriage celebration. In John 2:3, no reason is given for the wine's going out (hystereō).[60]

The basis of the haggadic interpretation "The last day was as good as the first" lies in the Hebrew of "180 days," which does not end in the expected plural יוֹמִים, but rather in the singular יוֹם: 180 "day."[61]

---

[55]Die Hochzeit 101.

[56]The Interpretation of the Fourth Gospel (Cambridge: Cambridge University, 1968) 297.

[57]See H. Windisch, "Die johanneische Weinregel (Joh. 2,10)" in ZNW 14 (1913) 248-57, as well as A. Smitmans, Das Weinwunder von Kana. Die Auslegung von Jo 2,1-11 bei den Vätern und heute (BGBE 6; Tübingen: Mohr, 1966) 27-28, 263.

[58]The Hebrew is found in Midrash Rabbah on Exodus and Esther (Hebrew; Jerusalem: Lewin-Epstein, 1960) 8b-9b.

[59]Est. Rab. 2/3 in Soncino 9.35-36, translated by M. Simon.

[60]The longer Greek variant reading has nothing to recommend it.

[61]See also A. Wünsche, Der Midrasch zum Buche Esther (Leipzig: Schulze, 1881) 18. J. Fürst translates: "Jedoch hier war es am letzten Tag so reichlich, wie am ersten" (84).

This, then, is the basis of the steward's remark in John 2:10. Bar Lufyeni began his marriage celebration with good wine and ended it with poor wine straight from the wine-press because he had no better. Yet Ahasuerus both began and ended his marriage feast with quality wine. The author of John 2:1-11 borrowed from this Esther tradition and expanded it with the statement "and when men have drunk freely."

The origin of the steward's remarks, however, can be ascertained even more exactly. In John 2:3 the term *hysterēsantos oinou* ("When the wine gave out") is translated into modern Hebrew in the United Bible Societies' edition of the "New Covenant" as כְּשֶׁחָסַר לָהֶם יַיִן.[62] In the LXX *hystereō* also usually translates חָסֵר. Four passages in the MT, especially the last, are of interest in regard to this Hebrew verb.

a) Cant 7:3 (Eng. 2) is the closest linguistic parallel to "wine lacking." It states: "Your navel is a rounded bowl that never *lacks* mixed wine *(mazeg)*." The latter, read as *mōzeg*, is interpreted in two rabbinic traditions of God, the "butler/steward of the world."[63] The targum on the next verse also mentions the Messiah son of David.[64] Early sources also note that the Song of Songs was sung at a marriage feast.[65] Cant 7:3 is also connected in rabbinic traditions to Ps 23:1, the great importance of which shall be shown in d) below.[66]

b) In 1 Kgs 17:14 Elijah tells the widow of Zarephath that "the cruse of oil shall not *fail*"; v. 16 states that it did not *fail*. Here, in a miracle, the motif of lacking/failing is emphasized.

c) The other biblical miracle story containing the motif of "lacking" is the manna from heaven given by God to the Israelites in the wilderness. Exod 16:18 states that "he that gathered little had no *lack*." This chapter is also related to Ps 23:5 in a rabbinic commentary on Exodus.[67]

d) The most important biblical passage in regard to חָסֵר, however, is Psalm 23, still today a favorite of both Jews and Christians. Verse one states: "The Lord is my shepherd, I shall not *want*." An example of this "not wanting" is given in v. 5: "Thou preparest a table before me in the presence of my enemies; thou anointest my head with oil, my cup *overflows* (רְוָיָה)." The LXX interprets the latter phrase as "thy cup makes me drunk/feel good like the best (wine)." The Greek verb here, *methyskō*, is the causal form of *methyō*, which is also found in John 2:10 ("When men have drunk freely" – RSV). Rab, a first

---

[62]Jerusalem: Yanetz, 1979, p. 237.

[63]See Cant. Rab. 7:3 § 1 (Soncino 9.281) and Jastrow 753, as well as Pesiq. R. 10/2 (Braude 1.172).

[64]English in S. Levey, *The Messiah: An Aramaic Interpretation* (Cincinnati: Hebrew Union College – Jewish Institute of Religion, 1974) 128.

[65]See *Str-B* 1.516 "aa."

[66]See Cant. Rab. 2:16 § 1 (Soncino 9.139) and 7:3 § 1 (Soncino 9.281).

[67]Exod. Rab. Beshallach 25/7 on Exod 16:4 (Soncino 3.308).

generation Babylonian Amora,[68] maintains that the measure of David's "cup" here will be 221 logs in the world to come, since the Hebrew letters of "overflows," רויה, denote this.[69] The head "anointed with oil" is also taken to refer to the Messiah, and the "prepared table" to the messianic banquet.[70]

Very early Tannaim also interpreted Psalm 23 of Israel's wilderness journey and God's care of the Israelites through the gift of manna from heaven. Most important in regard to John 2:1-11 is the narrative related by R. Judah (b. Ilai), a third generation Tanna:[71]

> As when a king is in a city, the city lacks (חֲסֵירָה) nothing, so "These forty years (שָׁנָה) the Lord your God has been with you; you have lacked (חָסַרְתָּ) nothing" (Deut 2:7). According to the custom of the world (בְּנוֹהַג שֶׁבָּעוֹלָם), when a man receives a guest, the first day he kills a calf for him; the second day a lamb; the third day a chicken; the fourth day he serves pulse to him; the fifth day he gives him even less, so that the first day is not like the last day for him. You could similarly maintain this (for Israel) in the wilderness. However, "You have lacked nothing" rather means: The first day was like the last.[72]

The same motif of "the first and last day being equally fine" when guest(s) are present is found here, as in Est. Rab. 2/3 above regarding Ahasuerus' feast in Esther 1. It is not based on the singular 180 "day" as there, but on forty "year." The motif of "lacking" plays a major role here, as in John 2:3, where the host does not provide adequately for his guests in the course of the seven-day wedding feast.[73] Finally, the phrase the steward of the feast employs in John 2:10 ("Every man...") is closely related to the phrase "according to the custom of the world," "ordinarily," found here.

Following this narrative in Midrash Psalms, R. Nehemiah also comments on Deut 2:7. Both he and R. Judah also comment five different times in Esther Rabbah on 1:1, 3 and 5.[74] There is thus no reason to doubt that R. Judah interpreted the 180 "day" of Esther 1:4 similarly, so that the motifs of "lacking" and "according to the custom of the world" became a part of Judaic haggada on Ahasuerus' wedding feast. Yet because of the similar "wine rule" in John 2:10, I

---

[68]Strack and Stemberger, *Einleitung* 90.

[69]See Midr. Ps. 23/6 on Ps 23:5 (Braude 1.333).

[70]Midr. Ps. 23/7 on Ps 23:5 (Braude 1.334).

[71]Strack and Stemberger, *Einleitung* 83.

[72]I have modified the translation of Braude in Midr. Ps. 23/3 on Ps 23:1 (1.328). Perhaps correct logically, he reverses the final sentence: "and the last day (in the wilderness for the children of Israel) was like the first." The Hebrew is found in S. Buber, *Midrasch Tehillim* (Vilna: Romm, 1891) 198.

[73]On a wedding feast as lasting seven days, see LXX Esther 2:18 and other sources cited in *Str-B* 1.517 "ee." The rabbis tend to merge the two separate banquets of Esther 1:3-4 and 5-8, so the reference to "seven days" in vv. 5 and 10 may also have suggested to them a marriage feast.

[74]Soncino 18, 24, 29, 38 and 39.

suspect that R. Judah b. Ilai, active ca. 130-160 C.E., received this from earlier teachers. His father, R. Ilai, a later second generation Tanna, often passed on the traditions of his own teacher R. Eliezer b. Hyrcanus, an older second generation Tanna.[75]

Finally, it should be noted that Philo of Alexandria, writing in the first half of the first century C.E., quotes in *Heres* 191 Exod 16:18 regarding the manna as distributed by the "divine Word" *(theios logos)*. In *Mut.* 114-15 he also speaks of the holy herd led by the "divine Word." Philo then quotes Ps 23:1, noting that God provides "a mass of good things" *(agatha...athroa)* for those who obey Him and do not rebel. In addition, he cites Ps 23:1 in *Agri.* 50, and then states in 51: "This hallowed flock He leads in accordance with right and law, setting over it His true Word and Firstborn Son who shall take upon him its government, like some viceroy of a great king."[76] He is God's "angel" of Exod 23:20 who will guide Israel through the wilderness to its home, Palestine.

Although Philo is in general non-eschatological and does not use the term "Messiah" at this point, it is hard to believe the latter is not meant here in regard to the manna tradition and Ps 23:1. If so, the connection of manna and Psalm 23:1-5 was not only Palestinian, but also known at an early time in Alexandria in Greek-speaking, diaspora Judaism. Many commentators believe the Fourth Evangelist derived his description of the "Logos" in his prologue in chapter one from that source, and the Messiah Jesus as the "good shepherd" in John 10:1-18 may also in part be based on Psalm 23.

F.   The Abundance and Quality of Wine at the Marriage Feast

1.   The Abundance

If one recalls the Persian love for overindulgence in wine while feasting mentioned in Section II, the description of wine consumption at Ahasuerus' banquet in Esther 1:7 is not astounding. Literally it is: "And the royal wine was much *(rav)*, like the hand of the king."

In Est. Rab. 2/12 on this verse, Dan 5:1 is cited regarding King Belshazzar, who made a great feast for 1000 of his lords. The midrash interprets the rest of the verse as his "drinking wine thousand-wise."[77] The rabbinic comment continues: "Yet here (regarding Ahasuerus) it is written, 'and the royal wine was

---

[75]Strack and Stemberger, *Einleitung* 79.

[76]English by F.H. Colson and G.H. Whitaker in LCL.

[77]Contrast Soncino 9.41, where the intention of the citation is misunderstood. J. Fürst in Wünsche, *Der Midrasch* 85, correctly translates: "und trank Wein entsprechend Tausend." The quantity is emphasized. This is also meant in b. Meg. 12b on Esther 1:12 (Soncino 71), where Vashti tells Ahasuerus: "Thou son of my father's steward, my father (Belshazzar) drank wine thousand-wise and did not get drunk, and that man (Ahasuerus) has become senseless with his wine." I have slightly modified M. Simon's translation.

as much as in the power of the king,' meaning according to the cups in the hand of the king." That is, Ahasuerus could drink even Belshazzar under the table, consuming more wine than he.[78] Esther 5:6 and 7:2 also emphasize his (and Haman's) drinking of wine.

The second targum on Esther 1:7 states that he who had drunk from one (wine) cup did not drink from it a second time; it was immediately taken away and a new one put in its place.[79] This recalls the Persian love of many drinking cups, also cited in Section II. Finally, Josephus in *Ant.* 11.188 states that it was a Persian custom to bring the guests wine continually.

The great amount of wine drunk at Ahasuerus' (wedding) feast provided part of the background for the 120 to 180 gallons (453 to 681 liters) of water[80] in John 2:6 which were changed to wine by Jesus at the wedding feast at Cana. A definite contrast is intended. Jesus the Messiah here provides far more wine than could ever be consumed at a seven-day Jewish wedding. He even provides more, or at least as much, as consumed at Ahasuerus' wedding to Vashti.[81] In reference to Ps 23:5, the measure of David's "overflowing" wine cup in the world to come will be 221 logs, or ca. 38 gallons, or 144 liters (see Section III, E, d). Yet more is already present in Jesus' activity at Cana. This "sign" indicates that Jesus, the "son of David," is the Messiah.

2. The Quality

Commenting on the word *rav* in Esther 1:7, Rab says: "This teaches that each one (of the guests at Ahasuerus' feast) was given to drink wine older than himself."[82] He interprets *rav*, "much," in its alternate meaning of "older." This

---

[78]See again Fürst, as in n.77.

[79]See Cassel, *Zweites Targum* 31, and *An Explanatory Commentary* 293, as well as Sulzbach, *Targum Scheni* 38. The tradition is also found in Midrash Abba Gorion on Esther 1:7. See S. Buber, *Haggadic Books on the Scroll of Esther* (Hebrew; Vilna: Romm, 1886) 10, and a German translation by A. Wünsche in *Aus Israels Lehrhallen* (Leipzig: Pfeiffer, 1907-09) II. 102. This is a wordplay on שׁוֹנִים as meaning "repeating," "again."

[80]RSV; this might be somewhat high. On the *metrētēs* (which only occurs in the NT here) as equal to about nine gallons or 39.39 liters, see BAGD 514. That would mean a total of ca. 108 to 162 gallons, or 473 to 709 liters.

[81]See also J. Bowman, *The Fourth Gospel and the Jews*. A Study in R. Akiba, Esther and the Gospel of John (PTMS 8; Pittsburgh: Pickwick, 1975) 163. Bowman deals with John 2:1-11 on pp. 161-63 and believes that the wedding feast at Cana shows indications of both Esther 1:5 and 2:18 (p. 161). There are, however, no indications of the latter. Unfortunately he does not analyze Judaic traditions on Esther 1. Nevertheless, he must be credited with being the first person I know of to perceive a relationship between John 2:1-11 and Esther (p. viii).

[82]See b. Meg. 12a (Sonc...no 70, with n.5).

is continued in Aggadat Esther on the same verse with the statement that if someone were forty years old, he was brought fifty-year-old wine to drink.[83]

Old wine was considered preferable to new. It is stated, for example, in b. Pes. 42b that old wine is one of those things "which are beneficial for the whole body." In b. Pes. 71a one "rejoices with clean garments and old wine."[84] In Luke 5:39, after mentioning the wedding guests and bridegroom, Jesus is reported as saying: "And no one after drinking old wine desires new; for he says, 'The old is good/better.'"

When the steward of the marriage feast tells the bridegroom in John 2:10 that he has kept the good wine until now, he thus means old, quality wine like that served at Ahasuerus' wedding feast.

G. The Steward of the Feast

In John 2:1-11 the "steward of the feast" *(architriklinos)* is mentioned three times in vv. 8-9. The commentators note that this word occurs only once in all of Judaic and Greek literature, and then in a third century C.E. work.[85] The author could have employed a more common expression such as *symposiarchos, oinoposiarchos, oinogeustēs*, or *archioinochoos* (LXX Gen 40:2, 9, 21; 41:9). He also did not choose *trikliniarchēs*, "director of a feast."[86] This leads one to believe that the term *architriklinos* was not just the reversal of the latter one, but an *ad hoc* creation by the author of John 2:1-11. I would propose the following reasons for this.

Esther 1:8 states regarding the banquet's taking place in the court of the garden of the king's palace (v. 5): the king ordered every רַב בֵּיתוֹ to do according to the will of each person. As G. Gerleman points out, this term is a *hapax legomenon* in the MT.[87] The LXX changes it into the plural, *oikonomoi*, "stewards," and the first targum employs here the Greek loanword *epitropos*,

---

[83]See S. Buber, *Aggadat Esther* (Cracow, 1897; with additions, Vilna 1925, and Jerusalem 1963-64) 12. In the second targum on the same verse, wine is given to each person according to his age, for example forty. This haggadic interpretation is a wordplay on שָׁנִים and "how old one is" *(ben...shanah)*.

[84]See Soncino 200 and 364. Cant. Rab. 1:2 § 3 (Soncino 9.35) states: "The longer wine matures in the jar, the better it becomes." In 'Abot 4:20 (Danby, *The Mishnah* 455), old wine is contrasted to that directly from the winepress. In m. B. Bat. 6:3 (Danby 374) "old wine" is one year old, "very old wine" two years old. In LXX Esther 1:7 "abundant and sweet wine" is mentioned, which may mean aged. For seven-year-old wine served at a circumcision feast, a portion of which is to be stored away for the son's wedding feast, see Deut. Rab. Vayelech 9/1 on Deut 31:14 (Soncino 7.156).

[85]See LSJ 253, referring to Heliodorus, *Erotici* 7.27.

[86]See LSJ 1819.

[87]*Esther* 61.

"administrator."[88] Since these terms do not adequately express in Greek the "head" position, I suggest the author of John 2:1-11 created his own word for רַב בֵּית.

The *rav* of "chief eunuch" and "chief guard" in Dan 1:3 and 2:14 is translated in the LXX, for example, by the prefix *archi-*, as in *architriklinos*. This shows that the author of John 2:1-11 could easily do the same for the *rav* of Esther 1:8.

In regard to the second part of the word *architriklinos*, it should be noted that the Greek *triklinon* (Latin *triclinium*) means "dining room." Josephus, for example, states in *Ant.* 20.192 that Agrippa II had a royal "dining room" in his Jerusalem palace, in which he reclined at meals and viewed the Temple.[89] The Greek term is also a loanword in rabbinic Hebrew.[90] In y. Sanh. 11:8(6),30c, for example, a *triklinon* is one of the rooms in the home of the bridegroom necessary to make a marriage valid.[91] Most important for our purposes, however, is Esther 7:8, which relates that Ahasuerus "returned from the palace garden to the place where they were drinking wine." For the latter phrase the second targum has טְרַקְלִינָא.[92] Ahasuerus' banquet site was thus also thought of as a *triklinon*.

Combining *archi-* as a known translation of *rav*, with the masculine form of *triklinon*, employed of the drinking site in Ahasuerus' palace, the author created *architriklinos* to express the Hebrew רַב בֵּית of Esther 1:8: "head waiter," "head butler," "steward of the feast."

Finally, in b. Meg. 12a on Esther 1:8, the expression אִישׁ-וָאִישׁ, "everyone," literally "a man and a man," is interpreted as referring to the men of the banquet as doing the will of Mordecai and Haman. Rashi says these two were the two "butlers" at Ahasuerus' banquet.[93] In regard to v. 8 it is related elsewhere that the Persian custom was to be forced to drink an immense cup of wine. Since no one was allowed to be an exception, the banquet guests bribed the "head waiter" (שַׂר הַמַּשְׁקִים) or their own butler (מְזוֹנָא) to get out of this.[94] These haggadic

---

[88]Grossfeld, *First Targum* 7 and 42.

[89]Noted by A. Schlatter, *Der Evangelist Johannes* (Stuttgart: Calwer, 1948) 70.

[90]See S. Krauss, *Griechische und lateinische Lehnwörter im Talmud, Midrasch und Targum* (Berlin: Calvary, 1899) 2.274.

[91]English in J. Neusner, *The Talmud of the Land of Israel,* 31: *Sanhedrin and Makkot* (Chicago: University of Chicago, 1984) 388. In his German translation, G. Wewers in *Talmud Yerushalmi, Sanhedrin* (Tübingen: Mohr, 1981) 317 notes the parallel in y. Ketub. 28d.

[92]See the passage as corrected in Jastrow, *A Dictionary* 554. Sulzbach, *Targum Scheni* 88, translates "Speisesaal."

[93]Soncino 70, with n.9.

[94]See Buber, *Aggadat Esther* 12; Panim Achérim 2 in Buber, *Haggadic Books* 59; and Yalqut Shim'oni §1048 on Esther 1:8, for the singular שַׂר. It derives from the "chief butler" of Pharaoh in Genesis 40-41. The plural שָׂרֵי is found in Abba Gorion and Leqach Tob (*Haggadic Books* 12 and 91). The term מְזוֹנָא, "wine-mixer,"

comments show that butlers, even a "head butler," were connected with Ahasuerus' feast and thus available to the author of John 2:1-11. They provided a model for his term *architriklinos*, found nowhere else in contemporary literature.

H. Ritual Purity at the Feast

Because of the great danger of Jewish accommodation to Hellenistic customs, the author of Daniel in the middle of the second century B.C.E. has his hero resolve in 1:8 to "not defile himself with the king's rich food, or with the wine which he drank." At King Belshazzar's feast, for example, "they drank wine, and praised the gods of gold and silver, bronze, iron, wood, and stone" (5:4). Daniel wanted no part of this idolatry. A Jew was later not permitted to drink non-Jewish wine, since it may have been used as a libation for an idol. In b. Hor. 11a, for example, "Our Rabbis taught: He who drinks wine of libation is considered an apostate."[95] For this reason a considerable portion of the Mishnah tractate Abodah Zarah deals with the wine, wine jars, and wine press of a non-Jew.[96]

Rabbinic comment on Ahasuerus' feast with much wine in Esther 1 mirrors the above concern for Jewish ritual purity, for food and drink as being "kosher." In Est. Rab. 2/13 on Esther 1:8, "no one was compelled," Rab says: "None compelled to drink wine of libation."[97] No Jew in attendance was thus forced indirectly to acknowledge a foreign god. The phrase "to do as every man desired" is interpreted in b. Meg. 12a, as noted above, to mean that the guests, Jews and non-Jews, "should do according to the will of Mordecai and Haman."[98] It is assumed that Mordecai will serve the Jewish guests only ritually pure foods.[99] Finally, R. Eliezer in Pirq. R. El. 49 cites Esther 1:4, continuing: "Every people who ate its food in impurity had its food provided in impurity, and every people who ate its food in purity had its food provided (according to the regulations of) purity," as Esther 1:8b is interpreted.[100]

"butler," is employed in 2 Targ. Esther 1:8 (Cassel, *Zweites Targum* 32). The LXX on Esther 1:8 already alludes to the Persian custom of forced heavy drinking mentioned above by saying that at Ahasuerus' feast it was *not* so. On רַב שָׁקֵי and רַב מְזוֹנַיָּא for "chief butler," see D. Rieder, *Targum Jonathan ben Uziel on Genesis and Exodus* (Jerusalem, 1984) 62-63 on Gen 40:2,9,20-21; 41:9.

[95] Soncino 79.

[96] See 2:3-4,6; and 4:8–5:11; as well as b. Abodah Zarah 30b-31a (Soncino 153).

[97] Soncino 9.41.

[98] Soncino 70.

[99] The first targum also differentiates between the wishes of Israelites and non-Jews here. See Grossfeld, *First Targum* 7 and 42.

[100] Friedlander 393. It is questionable whether this is R. Eliezer b. Hyrcanus, the second generation older Tanna. See also b. Meg. 13a on Esther 2:9 (Soncino 76), where Hegai gives Esther Jewish food to eat, and the second targum on the same

This motif of ritual purity is reflected in John 2:1-11.[101] Verse six states that "six stone jars were standing there, for the Jewish rites of purification." Since Jesus in v. 7 tells the servants to fill them with water, they up until then have been empty. They are storage jars.

It was usual for Jewish women to draw water for home use from a well with an open, "large pitcher/jug" (חַצְבָּא רַבָּא).[102] Such a vessel was employed so that as few trips as possible would have to be made back and forth to the well. This Aramaic term in the plural in Hebrew is חַצָּבִים גְּדוֹלִים and is employed in the Mishnah and Tosefta as (closed) "large storage vessels" for wine.[103]

Jastrow notes that the חָצָב could be either earthen or of stone.[104] Since stone vessels could not assume ritual impurity,[105] the author of John 2:1-11 states explicitly in v. 6 that the (open water) jars in the wedding house were of stone. They should be thought of as the "large vessels" mentioned above.

A. Schlatter forgets that these jars were first empty and suggests that such a great quantity of water was necessary for the ritual bath *(miqveh)* prescribed for after the bridal couple's first intercourse.[106] Yet such immersion pools were usually public ones and required at least some fresh, moving water.

Water was, however, needed for the ritual washing (not cleansing) of one's hands at a festive meal at the beginning and end, and after the various servings of wine.[107] Yet this amount was very small.[108]

Somewhat more water was necessary for mixing with wine. In t. Shab. 7:9 R. Aqiba's (wedding) banquet for his son is mentioned, at which the sage spoke a

---

verse (Cassel, *An Explanatory Commentary* 301), where Esther "did not want to taste of the wine which came from the house of the king."

[101]The Fourth Evangelist is interested in ritual (and moral) purity. See 3:25; 11:55; 13:10; 15:3; and 18:28. Vessels and purification also occur in 2 Tim 2:20 in a large house.

[102]See b. Betsa 30a (Soncino 154), commenting on m. Betsa 4:1, which states that the usual way of transporting wine jars was by carrying them in a basket or hamper. On this whole subject, see S. Krauss, *Talmudische Archäologie* (Leipzig: Fock, 1911) 1.81, 423-24; and 2.236.

[103]See m. Menach. 8:7; t. Menach. 9:10; m. Kelim 2:2; t. Kelim B. Qam. 2:2; and m. Kelim 9:8.

[104]*Dictionary* 494.

[105]See the sources cited in *Str-B* 2.406-07.

[106]*Der Evangelist Johannes* 68. Forty "seahs," or about sixty gallons (270 liters) of water, were required. See Danby, *The Mishnah* 732, and m. Miqv. 1:4. In 8:4 (p. 742) a woman has intercourse, then immerses herself. Yet contrast a bride's first intercourse in b. Yeb. 34b (Soncino 216), based on Lev 15:18.

[107]See y. Ber. 6:6,10d, citing t. Ber. 4:8, in C. Horowitz, *Der Jerusalemer Talmud. Berakhoth* (Tübingen: Mohr, 1975) 174. Cf. also the sources cited in *Str-B* 1.695–704 and 4.620-27.

[108]See the figures in *Str-B* 1.698 (one-fourth of a *log* each time).

blessing "over every single jug of wine which he opened."[109] Since wine was usually served with water in the proportion of one to two,[110] this required that a definite quantity of water be present for the seven days of the wedding, on which guests came and went. Yet the combined amounts needed for ritual hand-washing and wine-mixing for seven days would not even come close to the tremendous amount of water the six stone jars of John 2:6 indicate.

The author mentions the "purification of the Jews" because he was aware that Ahasuerus' wedding banquet was ritually pure for the Jews in attendance, and because he needed the six *empty* gigantic jars as a prop on the stage of his miracle/sign. They are to be "filled to the brim" to increase the effect on the reader/hearer.[111]

I. An Order

In Esther 1:8 the Hebrew states that King Ahasuerus "ordered every steward to do according to the will of each man." The LXX has for the first part of this: *epetaxen tois oikonomois poiēsai to thelēma autou,* "he ordered the house servants/stewards to do his will." In his paraphrase of this scene, Josephus in *Ant.* 11.188 employs the term *hoi diakonoi* and the verb *diakoneō.*

I suggest that this verse from Esther 1 provided the thought background for Mary's statement to the *diakonois,* house servants in John 2:5: "Whatever he says to you, do *(poiēsate)*." The author of John 2:1-11 simply considered the subject of *epetaxen* as "she" and not "he": "She (Mary) ordered the house servants to do his (Jesus') will." Since he desired direct address, however, the author clothed this thought in the exact words of another passage he knew well from the Bible.

In a desperate situation of no bread, the people of Egypt being extremely hungry, Pharaoh tells them in Gen 41:55 to go to Joseph, and "whatever he says to you, do." The LXX reads for the latter: *ho ean eipē hymin, poiēsate,* which is almost identical to John 2:5: *ho ti an legē hymin, poiēsate.* Here Pharaoh, although head of the country, steps back and puts Joseph in the foreground because he knows he can provide the bread. Although she is Jesus' mother and the first to arrive at the wedding (John 2:1), Mary also recedes into the

---

[109]See Neusner, *The Tosefta* 2.22, and the parallels cited by *Str-B* in 1.516. Jars of wine could usually be easily carried. Cf. m. Betsa 4:1 (Danby, *The Mishnah* 185).

[110]See the sources cited in *Str-B* 4.614, "h."

[111]For a wine jar's being "filled to the brim," see m. Menach. 8:7 (Danby 503), associated with "large storage vessels." The author of John 2:1-11 does not even consider how long it would take the house servants to go back and forth to the town well, or even a cistern, and fill the gigantic water vessels. For him, the only important thing is that it is Jesus who tells them to do this.

background, emphasizing her son's role. Her statement to the servants shows her confidence that her son can provide the wine that is lacking.[112]

If this reconstruction is basically true, it aids in explaining why John 2:5 is so strange in its context. The author employed a thought pattern from his source, Esther 1:8, and recast it in terms of another very similar passage from Genesis 41: there is no bread – there is no wine.

J. The Transformation

At Ahasuerus' feast, in the MT of Esther 1:7 the great amount of royal wine was served "in vessels of gold, and the vessels differing from the vessels." The Hebrew for "differing" here is שׁוֹנִים, the present participle of שָׁנָה.[113] With the preposition *min,* as here and elsewhere,[114] it indeed means "differing," as it is interpreted in the so-called "Lucianic" Greek text *(exalla).*[115] The beginning of 2 Targ. Est. 1:7 also states that he who drank from one cup did not drink from it again; it was taken from him and "another" provided in its place. This motif also occurs in other Esther midrashim.[116]

Yet the LXX already shows that other interpretations of שׁוֹנִים were made at an early date. It reads: "gold and silver cups, and a small cup of carbuncle worth 30,000 talents." This fantastically high value recalls the exquisitely fashioned Persian drinking cups of gold mentioned in Section II. The Greek term for "carbuncle" is *anthrakinos,* only occurring here. It probably means a stone which reflects like a mirror.[117] Josephus in *Ant.* 11.188 also mentions in this regard drinking cups made of "precious stone," and Est. Rab. 2/10 on Esther 1:7 certainly means this when it says that "these were vessels of finely cut crystal in which the face is beautifully mirrored as in gold."[118]

However, another interpretation of שׁוֹנִים was decisive for John 2:1-11. In 587 or 586 B.C.E. Nebuchadnezzar's army captured Jerusalem, sacked the Temple, and sent its vessels and much of the population into exile to Babylon.[119] Only under the later Persian King Cyrus, ca. 538 B.C.E., were these vessels returned to the Jerusalem Temple, whose rebuilding then began.[120]

---

[112]See also J. Breuss, *Das Kanawunder* (BibB 12; Fribourg: Schweizerisches Katholisches Bibelwerk, 1976) 24.

[113]See BDB 1039-40; Aramaic שְׁנָא, p. 1116.

[114]See Esther 3:8 and Dan 7:3,7,19, and 23-24.

[115]Clines, *The Esther Scroll* 218-19.

[116]See Cassel, *An Explanatory Commentary* 293, as well as Midr. Abba Gorion (Buber, *Haggadic Books* 10) and Aggadat Esther (Buber, 12) on 1:7.

[117]LSJ 140, with *anthrakion.*

[118]Soncino 9.40.

[119]On these vessels, see 2 Kgs 25:14-16; 2 Chr 36:18; and Jer 52:18-23.

[120]See Ezra 1:7-11; 1 Esdr 2:10-15; and Josephus, *Ant.* 11.10,14-15, with a list of vessels which greatly differs.

Although Ahasuerus actually reigned from 486-465 B.C.E., he is thought by the rabbis to have lived before Cyrus and thus also to be in possession of the Temple vessels.[121] For example, they have his queen Vashti say that she is a daughter of King Belshazzar, who in turn was a son of Nebuchadnezzar.[122]

According to Est. Rab. 2/11 on Esther 1:7, at his feast Ahasuerus "brought out his own vessels and those of Elam, and his own were finer than those of Elam."[123] Midr. Abba Gorion on this verse says the same was true for the vessels of the whole world.[124] Then Ahasuerus, calculating that the prophecy of Jeremiah (29:10; see also Dan 9:2) regarding the Jews' return to Jerusalem after seventy years in Babylon was now over and thus unfulfilled, also took out the Jerusalem Temple vessels for his guests. He knew that his father-in-law Belshazzar had done the same thing at his feast, yet because of a miscalculation was slain for this terrible act (Dan 5:1-30). However, he thought this could no longer happen to him; the seventy years were now definitely over.[125]

Est. Rab. 2/11 on Esther 1:7 continues regarding Ahasuerus:

> He brought his own vessels and those of the Temple, and they were finer and more beautiful than his. It was as if a matron had a beautiful maidservant, and whenever she looked at her maidservant her own color changed (הָיוּ פָּנֶיהָ מִשְׁתַּנּוֹת). So whenever his vessels were brought face to face with those of the Sanctuary, they changed color (הָיוּ מִשְׁתַּנִּין) and became (נַעֲשׂוֹ) like lead.[126]

This tradition of the extremely beautiful Persian drinking cups "changing" and "becoming like lead" in the presence of the Temple vessels, is also found in Aggadat Esther and Panim Achérim 2 on this verse,[127] and in Pirq. R. El.

---

[121]This is probably due to the sequence in Daniel of Nebuchadnezzar, Belshazzar (5:1), Darius the Mede (5:31), who is the son of Ahasuerus (9:1), and Cyrus in 10:1.

[122]In b. Meg. 12b (Soncino 71) and Est. Rab. 3/14 on Esther 1:12 (Soncino 9.54), Vashti accuses her husband of only being a servant of her father, (Belshazzar). In Dan 5:2 Belshazzar's father is in turn Nebuchadnezzar. In b. Meg. 10b (Soncino 58) Vashti is the daughter (which can also mean "granddaughter") of the wicked Nebuchadnezzar. In Est. Rab. Proem 12 (Soncino 9.17), Rab has the sequence Nebuchadnezzar, Evil-Merodach, Belshazzar, Vashti. For Vashti as the daughter of Belshazzar, son of Nebuchadnezzar, see Panim Achérim 2 (Buber 60-61) and Abba Gorion (Buber, 15-16), both on Esther 1:12. See also the second targum on this verse (Cassel, *Explanatory Commentary* 295).

[123]Soncino 9.40.

[124]Buber, *Haggadic Books* 10.

[125]See b. Meg. 11b in Soncino 65-66; 12a on Esther 1:7 in Soncino 70; and Est. Rab. 2/11 on the latter verse in Soncino 9.40-41.

[126]Soncino 9.40; I have slightly modified the English translation. The Hebrew is in Lewin-Epstein, 10a. A parallel is found in Midr. Abba Gorion on this verse (Buber 9-10), and in Yalqut Shim'oni on Esther §1048.

[127]See Buber, *Aggadat Esther* 12, and his *Haggadic Books* 59.

49.[128] The first targum also states here that King Ahasuerus' vessels "were changed in their appearance to the likeness of lead, and in the presence of the Temple vessels they were transformed."[129]

This is a haggadic wordplay on שׁוֹנִים not in the sense of "differing from," but "changing." It in turn is derived from the Belshazzar drinking feast just alluded to, where the king employs the Temple vessels and misuses them for wine libations to other gods (Dan 5:4,23). This behavior leads to the famous handwriting on the wall, in which Belshazzar is found "wanting" (חַסִּיר; LXX hysterousa) in v. 27, a verb also occurring in John 2:3.[130]

Out of fear, the king's countenance "changed" (Aramaic שְׁנָא) in 5:6,9-10.[131] The word for "countenance" here is ziw, which is actually "brightness," "splendor," "glory."[132]

The midrashim and the first targum on Esther 1:7 can thus maintain that all the royal "glory" of King Ahasuerus (v. 4), all the exquisitely beautiful, golden drinking cups of Persia, lose their own glory and splendor in the sight of the Jerusalem Temple vessels. Indeed, before the latter they turn to dull lead.

The author of John 2:1-11 certainly knew of the above haggadic tradition on שׁוֹנִים in Esther 1:7, and of its origin in the Belshazzar feast, the background of that tradition. Out of it he created a new narrative of a wedding feast at Cana, where, because wine was "lacking," Jesus "changed" water into wine.

The Greek of "water now become wine" in John 2:9 is *to hydōr oinon gegenēmenon.* The perfect passive participle of *ginomai,* "to become," "to come into a new state of being," is employed here.[133] In 4:46, the Fourth Evangelist refers back to Cana in chapter two, where Jesus "had *made* the water wine." Here the active of *poieō,* "to do," "to make," is employed for the same event. Both are good translations of the niphal (passive), נַעֲשָׂה לְ, "to become," and the qal (active), עָשָׂה, "to make."[134] This word is employed in the midrashim cited above of Ahasuerus' vessels "having been made," their "becoming" like lead in the presence of the Temple vessels. I suggest that the passive Greek participle in John 2:9 is due to this niphal (passive) form.

One more observation on Daniel 5 is of relevance here. The author of John 2:1-11 knew of haggadic comment on Esther 1:7 in which Ahasuerus compared

---

[128]Friedlander 393.

[129]Grossfeld, *First Targum* 7 and 41.

[130]When Josephus retells this narrative in *Ant.* 10.232-44, he strongly emphasizes Belshazzar's "blaspheming" God by employing the Lord's vessels for drinking. He had even stored them in his own pagan temple.

[131]For this expression, see also 3:19 and 7:28.

[132]BDB 1091, and Jastrow, *A Dictionary* 392, with an example of a son's looks changing.

[133]LSJ 349.

[134]Jastrow, *A Dictionary* 1124-25.

himself to his father-in-law Belshazzar in Daniel 5. He also was aware of Ahasuerus' own vessels' "changing," a term also derived from that chapter. Having it in mind, he borrowed a phrase from the same chapter in order to describe the action of one of his figures in John 2:9: "when the steward of the feast tasted the water now become wine...."

In Greek the latter is: *hōs de egeusato ho architriklinos to hydōr oinon gegenēmenon.* This imagery is dependent on Dan 5:2, which states that at his great feast, drinking wine, King Belshazzar, *"when he tasted the wine,* commanded that the vessels of gold and silver which Nebuchadnezzar his father had taken out of the Temple in Jerusalem be brought in." This is the only occasion in the MT and the LXX of "tasting wine."[135] The Aramaic here is בִּטְעֵם חַמְרָא, literally "in (his) taste of (the) wine." The phrase is lacking in the LXX, but in Theodotion it is translated literally: *en tē geusei tou oinou.* The author of John 2:1-11 made his own translation of this Aramaic phrase, which is just as good Greek.

K. Showing Glory

Mention was made in Section II of the Persian rulers' treasure-houses in the palace at Susa. There countless objects of tribute from the entire empire were stored and displayed.

This motif is also found in rabbinic comment on Esther 1:4. The verse states that King Ahasuerus at his (wedding) banquet "showed the riches of his royal glory (כְּבוֹד) and the splendor (יְקָר) and pomp of his majesty" for 180 days.[136]

In regard to this passage Exod. Rab. Va'era 9/7 on Exod 7:12 relates: "Our Sages have said: He (Ahasuerus) showed them six collections of treasure every day and not two of them were alike."[137] Then various rabbis comment on the content of the treasures he "showed" the wedding guests.[138] There were six treasures each day because of the six different Hebrew nouns from "riches" to "majesty" in Esther 1:4. The first targum on this verse also speaks of all the wealth Ahasuerus inherited and states that through it "his glory (יְקָרֵיהּ)

---

[135]Jer 48:11 does not mention wine, only the lees of a vessel.

[136]For the Hebrew "at his showing" (בְּהַרְאֹתוֹ), the LXX employs *to deixai,* and the "Lucianic" Greek text (Clines, *The Esther Scroll* 218-19) *to epideichthēnai,* and Josephus in *Ant.*11.186 the noun *epideixis.* The hiphil infinitive in 1:11 and 4:8 is also translated by *deixai* in the LXX.

[137]Sconcino 3.124.

[138]This tradition is also found in Est. Rab. 2/1 on Est 1:4 (Soncino 9.33), where it derives from the "School of Jannai and Hezekiah." There (Hebrew, *Midrash Rabbah* 8a) נִיסִין, "miracles," is a printing error for גִּיסִין, "spoils, heaped up treasures" (Jastrow 240). See also Midr. Abba Gorion on Est 1:4 (Buber, *Haggadic Books* 9); Panim Achérim 2 on 1:4 (Buber 58, with תִּיסְבָּרִיּוֹת; Jastrow 1682); and the second targum on this verse (Cassel, *Explanatory Commentary* 293).

intensified."[139] Not to be outdone, Vashti also opened six treasuries at her feast, as "*Also* Queen Vashti" is interpreted in Est. Rab. 3/9 on Esther 1:9.[140]

I suggest that this motif of "showing glory" from Esther 1:4 influenced the formulation of the phrase "And he (Jesus) revealed his glory" in John 2:11 in regard to the miracle or sign at Cana. The LXX usually employs *doxa* of the Hebrew כָּבוֹד, yet at Esther 1:4; 6:3; and Dan 2:37 it also translates יְקָר, so. Both Hebrew terms occur in Esther 1:4, where Ahasuerus showed both his glory and splendor at his wedding feast. Jesus is presented as also showing his glory at a wedding feast, in Cana.

The Greek verb *phaneroō* employed in John 2:11 of Jesus' "revealing" his glory is found only once in the entire LXX, and only once in the other three gospels (Mark 4:22). Yet it occurs a total of nine times in the Fourth Gospel. If 2:1-11 are not from the Gospel writer, but from a source he took over, I suggest that the Evangelist changed the usual form *edeixe*, "he showed," which he found in his source, to a favorite term, *ephanerōsen*. He wanted to emphasize Jesus' very close relationship with God, that Jesus' deeds were wrought in God (3:21). For him, it is Jesus and he alone who reveals God's name to mankind (17:4-6). The "sign" at Cana thus points to Jesus as being in a very special relationship to God.

This suggestion is corroborated in the MT, where "showing glory" occurs only twice. In Exod 33:18 Moses says to God at Mt. Sinai: "I pray thee, show me thy glory." The other passage is Deut 5:24, where the Israelites tell Moses in regard to the Sinai revelation: "Behold, the Lord our God has shown us his glory."

For the Fourth Evangelist, when Jesus "shows his glory," it partly recalls the Sinai event at which the Lord (God) showed his glory, at which He revealed himself. Yet for the Evangelist, Jesus' glory goes back even further, for it is from the Father (1:4), with whom the Word has been since the very beginning (1:1).

❊ ❊ ❊

The eight motifs and verbal similarities analyzed in sections D–K between Ahasuerus' marriage feast and the wedding feast at Cana can be questioned individually. Cumulatively, however, they offer very strong evidence that the author of John 2:1-11 based much of his narrative on Judaic haggadic traditions concerning Esther 1:1-8.

---

[139]Grossfeld, *The First Targum* 6 and 41.
[140]Soncino 9.51-52.

IV. THE LEGITIMATE USE OF RABBINIC TRADITIONS ON ESTHER 1

Before discussing the earliest ascertainable content and the meaning of the sign/miracle now found in John 2:1-11, several remarks are appropriate in regard to the use of rabbinic materials cited in Section III.

Recent research on the Scroll of Esther points to various stages within the development of the book. The LXX, while basically following what is today called the Masoretic Text, at many points paraphrases or inserts motifs not found in the Hebrew, such as Ahasuerus' feast in chapter one as a wedding feast. It also incorporates six "Additions" to Esther, probably primarily designed to make the Scroll more acceptable as part of the "canon." As is well-known, for example, the term "God" never appears in the MT of Esther. These additions were certainly made before the first century C.E. The so-called "Lucianic" Greek text is not dependent on the LXX and at times presupposes a Hebrew text differing from the MT. It is also from before the first century C.E.[141]

The earliest other datable use of the Book of Esther is found in Josephus, who writes at the end of the first century C.E. Aramaic-speaking, born in Jerusalem ca. 37-38 C.E. of priestly descent, and having grown up there (*Vita* 5-8), he retells the Esther narrative in *Ant.* 11. He is not only acquainted with the Additions in the LXX, he also betrays good knowledge of haggadic material, such as his description of the vessels employed at Ahasuerus' feast in Esther 1, and the Persian custom of forcing banquet guests to drink wine continually (11.187-88).

In b. Meg. 10b-17b and in Esther Rabbah, many later rabbis, the "Amoraim," are cited. Yet the number and frequency of the earlier rabbis, the Tannaim, cited is also impressive. On Esther 1:1-9, for example, Rabbis Aquilas and Aqiba (T2); Joshua b. Karchah, Judah b. Ilai, Nehemiah, Meir and Simeon b. Yochai (T3); Eliezer b. Yose, Nathan and Judah the Prince (T4); and Chiyya b. Abba (T5) are quoted, as are a number of "baraithas," tannaitic traditions not found in the Mishnah. Finally, the term "our rabbis taught," which occurs a number of times, also points to early traditions.

In light of all these materials, it may be legitimately assumed that haggadic comment on the very popular Scroll of Esther began at a very early time (LXX and the "Lucianic" Greek text) and was continued into the first century C.E. (Josephus) and beyond. The narrative of the wedding at Cana in John 2:1-11 is found in the Fourth Gospel, which is usually dated somewhere between 80-100 C.E.[142] Even if the final editing of the targums and midrashim on Esther was

---

[141]See Clines, *The Esther Scroll* 69-72, and *passim*, as well as Moore, *Studies* LXVII, 521-28 and 583-94.
[142]J. Becker, *Das Evangelium des Johannes* (ÖTNT; Gütersloh: Mohn, 1979) 1.50-51.

centuries later, and even though they also show much definitely later development of earlier haggadic traditions, nevertheless they *also* contain materials which go back to the earliest Tannaim. If motifs and even phraseology found in John 2:1-11 are very similar to some of the rabbinic materials now found in the Esther midrashim, it is thus legitimate to assume that the former are part of an early stream of tradition.

V. THE CONTENT AND MEANING OF THE MIRACLE/SIGN

In Section III, I pointed out motifs and phraseology from Judaic traditions on Ahasuerus' feast in Esther 1 which provide the background of many of the motifs and phrases in John 2:1-11. Yet because many scholars consider the latter narrative to have been part of a "signs source" employed by the Fourth Evangelist, in order to determine its original contents and meaning it is first necessary to analyze it by itself, then as part of a hypothetical "signs source," and finally in the context of the entire gospel.

A. The Story by Itself

It cannot be proved with absolute certainty that the Fourth Evangelist did not himself create the narrative of John 2:1-11. Along with most commentators, however, I do not consider him to be the author. Under the assumption that "John" found the story in a source and incorporated it into his gospel, I suggest that the following phrases are from him.

a)   The phrase "O woman, what do you have to do with me?" in v. 4 is similar to Jesus' words to Peter in 21:22, "What is that to you?" It appears to be Johannine, that is, from the Evangelist or the author of chapter 21, if they are not the same.[143]

b)   "My hour has not yet come" in v. 4b is definitely from the Evangelist, who emphasizes this motif in regard to Jesus' death at a number of points.[144]

In the original story, v. 4 in its entirety was probably missing. Mary's remark in v. 3, "They have no wine," was followed with something like: "Help them." After this, v. 5 would have continued: "His mother *then* said...."

c)   "Of the Jews" in v. 6 also derives from the Evangelist, who seeks to explain to non-Jews reading his gospel whose purification is meant. The motif

---

[143]The most recent analysis of this phrase is that of A. Maynard, "*ti emoi kai soi*" in *NTS* 31 (1985) 582-86. His discussion of the Synoptic materials is helpful in pointing to Jesus' now "moving and living on a divine level where he has no filial relationship" to Mary (p. 585). For the pattern involved here, see C. Giblin, "Suggestion, Negative Response, and Positive Action in St. John's Portrayal of Jesus (John 2.1-11; 4.46-54; 7.2-14; 11.1-44)" in *NTS* 26 (1980) 197-211.
[144]See 7:6,8,30; 8:20; 12:23; 13:1; 17:1.

of purification, however, is probably original, as it is emphasized in haggadic traditions on Esther 1.

d) The words in v. 9, "and did not know where it came from (though the servants who had drawn the water knew)," also derive from the Evangelist. His use of such "parentheses," including phrases with a double meaning, is well-known.[145]

e) The term "first" in v. 11 would also have been lacking in the original, which could have read: "This sign Jesus did at...." The word either derives from the Evangelist, or possibly from a "signs source" (see below).

f) The verb "manifested" in v. 11 is also from the Evangelist, as noted in Section III, K. The source most probably had "showed."

Aside from these five relatively minor additions and one change, the original narrative was basically as it is now found in 2:1-11. It is based on similar material in haggadic traditions on Ahasuerus' wedding feast. In the latter there are also a bridegroom, servants, a head waiter, and guests; there is no lack of wine – the very opposite is the case; there is an interest in ritual purity at the banquet; there is a parallel to the saying in v. 10; a transformation takes place; and Ahasuerus also shows his glory.

The author of John 2:1-11 basically retained the characters he found in the Esther 1 traditions available to him. He too has a bridegroom, servants, a head waiter, and guests (Mary, Jesus and the disciples). The major change on his part was his introduction of the figures of Mary and Jesus. Mary is basically a prop. She is there simply because someone has to make Jesus aware of the lack of wine. Only then can Jesus perform a sign and show his glory. The author expanded the motif of ritual purity already in his source into six stone jars capable of containing tremendous amounts. These he also needed as a prop for the fantastic amount of water Jesus was to transform into wine.

***

If the above construction is basically correct, we learn a) a number of things about the original narrative which are true, and b) many more things maintained by scholars about it which are not true.

(a) First, the early Jewish hearer or reader, who annually celebrated Purim by reading the Scroll of Esther, would certainly have noted allusions in the wedding story of Cana to Jewish haggadah on Ahasuerus' magnificent wedding feast in Esther 1. When hearing or reading that this was a "sign" of Jesus, he would also immediately have been reminded of the Scroll of Esther, *the* biblical book of "signs." The miracle of God's rescuing his people from total destruction

---

[145]See 1:15; 3:4; 4:2,9b; 6:6; and 7:22. I leave the question open as to whether a later "redactor" has added some of these.

according to Judaic tradition was the last "sign" in the Bible. Jesus' transformation of water into wine at Cana was to be seen as a continuation of this sign tradition. If so, it points to Jesus as a very special figure.

The wedding setting of the Cana miracle also suggests that the messianic period has already begun through Jesus' activity, for the days of the Messiah were thought to be like a wedding.

The wedding feast of Ahasuerus is also compared in Judaic sources with the messianic banquet. Through his transforming a fantastic amount of water into wine at Cana, Jesus is thought of as already giving a foretaste of the latter banquet. There, the messianic shepherd will cause the participant's cup not to lack anything; indeed, he or she will receive the best wine. The quantity of Jesus' wine at Cana is not only comparable to that of the extremely wealthy King Ahasuerus; it also exceeds that of David's cup, which itself "overflows" – in great abundance (Psalm 23). For the Jew, Jesus is here pictured as the "son of David," the Messiah.

Finally, at Cana Jesus shows his glory, just as Ahasuerus showed his glory at his wedding feast. Rabbinic sources also speak of the Messiah's "glory." In Midr. Ps. 21/1 on Ps 21:1-2, for example, the statement is made: "What can 'His rest shall be glory' (Isa 11:10) mean except that God will bestow a portion of His supernal glory upon the king Messiah."[146] The same motif is repeated in the midrash on Ps 21:6.[147] The Messiah's "glory" may be a very old motif, for the Psalms of Solomon, dating from the first century B.C.E., state in 17:30 that the son of David, Israel's king (v. 21), the "Lord's Messiah" (v. 32), will "glorify the Lord in (a place) prominent (above) the whole earth." Indeed, nations will "come from the ends of the earth to see his (the Messiah's) glory" (v. 31).[148] In addition, in 1 Enoch 49:2, the Elect One's "glory is forever and ever." In 48:10 he is the Messiah of the Lord of Spirits, called the Chosen One in v. 6 and the Son of man in v. 2. This section of 1 Enoch is at the latest from the first century C.E.[149]

Jesus' "showing his glory" at Cana thus also describes him for the early Jewish hearer or reader as the Messiah, who receives his glory from God. It is no wonder the author states at John 2:11: "and his disciples believed in him." This was the main purpose of the author's creating the entire narrative of 2:1-11.

---

[146]Braude 1.293. The author, R. Acha, is perhaps a fourth generation Palestinian Amora (Strack and Stemberger, *Einleitung* 98).

[147]Braude 1.295-96.

[148]For the text and dating, see R. Wright in *The Old Testament Pseudepigrapha*, ed. J. Charlesworth (Garden City, New York: Doubleday, 1985) 2.667 and 640-42. Isa. 55:5 is in the background of the text.

[149]See E. Isaac in *The Old Testament Pseudepigrapha* 1.35-36 and 7, which also notes R. H. Charles' dating of 105-64 B.C.E. I owe several references here to R. Brown, *The Gospel According to John*, I-XII (AB 29; Garden City, New York: Doubleday, 1966) 105.

The hearer/reader is also encouraged to believe that Jesus is the long-awaited Messiah.

(b) Many things, however, are also *not* true about John 2:1-11.

1. The narrative is not "the account of an actual event," as maintained by J.N. Sanders,[150] J. Bernard,[151] and W. Barclay.[152] It is, however, "true" in a religious sense. The author created it to persuade others to believe in Jesus as the true Messiah.

2. The narrative is also not taken over from a pagan Dionysos wine epiphany legend, as R. Bultmann claimed.[153] Rather, the author created it on the basis of Judaic haggadah on Esther 1. In Section VI, I shall briefly discuss the Dionysos legend in relation to the addressees of the entire gospel.

3. In Philo, *Som.* 2.183 (27) God's cup-bearer is identified with the truly great high priest who pours out the drink-offering of wine, himself. In 249 (37) the Word, the cup-bearer of God and master of the feast, is also stated to be the content of the cup of true gladness, in Jerusalem. The latter passage has also been associated with *All. Leg.* 3.82 (26), where Melchizedek in Jerusalem should offer wine instead of water.

These passages may have influenced the Fourth Gospel's description of the "high priestly prayer" in chapter 17, in which on the eve of his crucifixion Jesus describes his going to the Father, as well as the description of Jesus as the high priest in Hebrews, who offers up himself. Yet they are not visible in John 2:1-11 whatsoever.[154] At the most, the association of the Word and Psalm 23, as noted in Section III, may play a role here.

4. B. Lindars believes John 2:10 "preserves the conclusion of a genuine parable of Jesus," which through expansion was given a narrative setting.[155] R. Fortna had made a similar suggestion earlier.[156] There is good reason, however, for v. 10 not being present in the Synoptic tradition as a saying or parable of Jesus. The author of 2:1-11 borrowed it not from Jesus, but from Judaic haggadah on Esther 1.

---

[150]*The Gospel According to St. John* (Black's 4; London: Black, 1968) 115.

[151]*The Gospel According to St. John* (ICC; Edinburgh: Clark, 1958) 80.

[152]*The Gospel of John* (Philadelphia: Westminster, 1956) 1.81: "it is clearly an eye-witness account."

[153]*Das Evangelium des Johannes* (Meyer 2; Göttingen: Vandenhoeck & Ruprecht, 1964) 83. Barrett, *The Gospel* 161, also believes it "may be of Hellenistic origin."

[154]Against C.H. Dodd, *The Interpretation of the Fourth Gospel* (Cambridge: Cambridge University, 1968) 298-99, who calls these passages the "best clue" to 2:1-11 and cites other references to Philo.

[155]*The Gospel of John* (NCB 4; London: Oliphants, 1977) 126-28.

[156]*The Gospel of Signs* (SNTSMS 11; Cambridge, England: Cambridge University, 1970) 34.

5. There are also no indications that the marriage at Cana was a Pentecost meditation, as maintained by J. Grassi.[157] Rather, it is ultimately related to the festival of Purim.

6. D. Clark has attempted to present John 2:1-11 as one of the seven signs he sees in Wisdom of Solomon 11-19.[158] It is rather dependent on the Scroll of Esther.

Other, older suggestions as to the origin of John 2:1-11 are listed by H. Strathmann in his John commentary.[159] All of them are also to be rejected in light of the narrative's derivation from Judaic haggadic traditions on Esther 1.

B. The "Signs Source"

Ever since Bultmann's John commentary, there has been much effort to ascertain a "signs source" in the gospel, beginning with the wedding at Cana (2:11 – "the first of his signs"), continuing with 4:46-53 (v. 54: "This was now the second sign"), and extending further. More recent scholarship on John has centered on the number and content of these signs.

If 2:1-11 became a part of such a collection of miracles, it assumes other dimensions from those just noted in section A. Since it is emphasized in 10:41 that John the Baptist did *no* sign, it seems probable that after his death his followers were part of the audience to which such a "mission tract" was addressed.[160]

Secondly, the signs source can only have arisen in a Jewish-Christian atmosphere, and its author(s) and audience "seem to have been bilingual."[161] This would fit the description I have proposed in Section III: the creator of John 2:1-11 not only was a Jewish Christian, but was also aware of both Hebrew and Aramaic, as well as Greek (LXX, perhaps also Philo on Psalm 23) haggadic traditions on Esther 1.

Finally, the number of miracles in the signs source is controversial. Assuming with most commentators that John 21 is a later addendum to the Gospel, I would with others count seven: 2:1-11; 4:46-54; 5:1-9; 6:1-14; 6:15-25; 9:1-8; and 11:1-45. This has nothing to do with seven as the "perfect number" in Judaism, but rather exclusively with "signs."

---

[157]"The Wedding at Cana (John II 1-11): A Pentecostal Meditation?" in *NT* 14 (1972) 131-36.

[158]"Signs in Wisdom and John" in *CBQ* 45 (1983) 201-09, especially 206.

[159]*Das Evangelium nach Johannes* (NTD 4; Göttingen: Vandenhoeck & Ruprecht, 1959) 59.

[160]See Fortna, *The Gospel of Signs* 225, as well as D.M. Smith, "The Milieu of the Johannine Miracle Source: A Proposal," in R. Hamerton-Kelly and R. Scroggs, eds., *Jews, Greeks and Christians* (Leiden: Brill, 1976) 164-80, especially 176-78.

[161]Fortna, *The Gospel of Signs* 223.

All of Pirq. R. El. 52 deals with the "seven wonderful things" (דְּבָרִים מוֹפְתִים) which "have been done in the world, the like of which have not been created."[162] The word מוֹפֵת employed here is another term for "miracle."[163] The fifth of the miracles also has to do with "transformation," as at Cana. It describes the waters of the sea being "changed" into dry land at the Exodus event. It should be noted that when the Israelites saw this "great work," they "believed in the Lord and in his servant Moses" in Exod 14:31. The Palestinian targum has "signs" (נִיסִין) here, as well as: "they believed in the name of the Word *(Mēmra)* of the Lord."[164] The same reaction to Jesus' transformation of water into wine, his first "sign," is found in John 2:11.

Certainly intended as a parallel to the above seven miracles, the late midrash "Pirqé Mashiach" relates that in the final time, when the prophet Elijah appears, the Israelites will not believe that he is indeed Elijah, and the person with him is the King Messiah. Thus the prophet asks them: "Perhaps you wish (lit. 'seek')[165] that I do signs (אוֹתוֹת) for you like Moses?" When they affirm this, he performs seven נִיסִין, "signs."[166] These are designed to show that he definitely is Elijah, and the King Messiah is also the King Messiah.

While the latter midrash is very late, it shows that a similar series of seven signs could have been formed earlier by Jewish Christians to be parallel with the "seven miracles which have been done in the world." All the other six signs in the Fourth Gospel which are listed above have parallels in the Synoptics. Only Jesus' first sign, the transformation of water at Cana, does not. I suggest that it was placed at the beginning of the series of seven in order to show continuity with the last sign done in the Hebrew Bible, the miraculous rescue of the Jews from total destruction described in Esther. This motif of continuity would have appealed to the intended audience, Jews whom their fellow Jewish Christians sought to convince that Jesus is the Messiah.

---

[162]Friedlander, *Pirke de Rabbi Eliezer* 420-27. On p. 420, n. 1, he cites a parallel in Yalqut. I employ the Hebrew edition *Pirqe Rabbi Eliezer* (Jerusalem: Eshkol, 1973) 208-12.

[163]Jastrow, *A Dictionary* 746.

[164]See Rieder, *Targum Jonathan ben Uziel* 103, as well as Neofiti 1, including the marginal reading ("M"), in A. Díes Macho, *Neophyti 1*. Targum palestinense, ms. de la Biblioteca Vaticana. Tomo II, Éxodo (Madrid: Consejo superior de investigaciones cientificas, 1970) 95 and 449.

[165]See, for example, Mark 8:11-12 par.; Luke 23:8; and 1 Cor 1:22.

[166]See the Hebrew in A. Jellinek, *Bet ha-Midrasch* (Jerusalem: Wahrmann, 1967³) 3.72, and the parallel tradition in the "Pirqe R. Yoshiyyahu" in 6.115-16. Wünsche translates the first in *Aus Israels Lehrhallen* 3.133-34.

C. John 2:1-11 in Its Context

In Section V, A. I have described the six additions and changes the author of the Fourth Gospel[167] most probably made to the narrative he found in his source, whether the latter was independent or already in a signs source. Here I would also like to emphasize its importance in the present context, and in regard to the theme of "being greater than...."

1. The Context

In his prologue, the Evangelist in 1:14 states that Jesus "the Word became flesh and dwelt among us, and we have beheld his glory, glory as of the only Son of the Father, he (the Word) being full *(plērēs)* of grace and truth." In regard to the latter motif of "fulness," v. 16 continues by asserting that "from his fulness *(plērōma)* we have all received, grace upon grace," that is, abundantly. Jesus' "fulness," the abundance of his gifts, first becomes visible to the reader of the Gospel in 2:1-11, with its superabundance of wine.

Secondly, Jesus' promise to Nathanael in 1:50 that he will see "greater things" *(meizō)* than his own miraculous calling is also first illustrated by 2:1-11.

Thirdly, the Son's glory, deriving from the Father (1:14), is also first manifested in 2:1-11. This the Fourth Evangelist emphasizes by changing the probable verb "showed" of his source to one of his favorite terms, "to manifest."

Finally, following 2:1-11 Jesus in 13-25 goes up to Jerusalem to celebrate the Passover. While there he cleanses the Temple, which in the Synoptic tradition is also done before Passover. Yet it is at the very end of the Synoptic gospel narrative, the only time Jesus visits Jerusalem (Mark 11:15-17 par.). Most commentators therefore believe John 2:13-25 is misplaced, or it is intended to signify Jesus' going up several times to Jerusalem during his adult ministry. While the latter may be true anyway, I suggest another reason why the Evangelist placed the passage here. As a Jewish Christian himself, he knew that 2:1-11 was based on Esther 1, that is, the Scroll which was required reading at the festival of Purim. The latter was celebrated in the last Hebrew month, on the 14th-15th of Adar (Esther 9:18-19), approximately March. The next Hebrew month is Nisan (Esther 3:7), in which Passover is celebrated, in March-April. The Fourth Evangelist, at least here, was also considerate of his (Jewish) readers' calendar.

A possible corroboration of the above suggestion is the fact that only the Fourth Evangelist mentions Hanukkah, another non-pilgrim, post-biblical festival, in 10:22.[168]

---

[167]It is simply too complicated for this discussion also to consider the possibility of a "final redactor" who may also have been at work here.

[168]The order might then be Purim in 2:1-11; Pessach in 2:13-25; Shevuot (Weeks) in 4:5-42 (the "first-fruits" imagery and "harvesting" in vv. 35-38); Sukkot

2. Being Greater Than

When Jesus changed a tremendous amount of water into wine at Cana, he showed that he was greater than Ahasuerus, thought to be the wealthiest non-Jew of all. The wine at the latter's own marriage feast was only abundant – "much." Jesus' wine was superabundant, as indicated by the content of the six stone jars.

The motif of Jesus' "being more than" is already emphasized in the Synoptics. The wealthiest Israelite in Judaic tradition was Solomon. "All of his glory" is also mentioned by Jesus in Matt 6:29 // Luke 12:27. In Judaic midrashim, Ahasuerus' royal throne in Esther 1:2 was considered either Solomon's or a copy of it, for he sought to imitate Solomon's wealth and glory.[169] Yet Jesus says of himself in Matt 12:42 (// Luke 11:31): "Behold, something greater than Solomon is here." He maintains the same in regard to Jonah in Matt 12:41 (// Luke 11:32).

In the Gospel of John, Jesus is presented as not only more than Ahasuerus. He is also more than, he supersedes: Moses,[170] Abraham,[171] Jacob,[172] the prophets,[173] Elijah,[174] Elisha,[175] and John the Baptist,[176] thought by many to be Elijah, who was to return in the end-time. In this respect the Fourth Evangelist is like the author of Hebrews. As in the Gospel of John, the latter begins by saying God used to speak through the prophets. Yet now he has spoken through Jesus, through whom he created the world, who reflects God's glory and is superior to the angels (Heb 1: 1-4). Jesus also has more glory than Moses (3:3).

(Tabernacles) in 7:2; Hanukkah in 10:22; and Passover again as of 11:55. Then only the Passover of 6:4 interrupts the regular sequence. The author was unable to fit it in at 2:13-25, or as of 11:55, for there he already had a very long discourse, the Farewell Address of Jesus.

[169] See Est. Rab. 1/12 on Est 1:2 (Soncino 9.26) and the many other sources on this theme cited in Ginzberg, *Legends* 4.368 and 6.452-54. Solomon's and Ahasuerus' world-wide reigns are also compared. See the sources cited above in Part III on "from India to Ethiopia" in Est. 1:1.

[170] See John 1:17; 4:5; 5:46; 6:32; 7:23; 9:28-29.

[171] Chapter 8, especially v. 53: "Are you greater than our father Abraham?"

[172] John 4:12 has the Samaritan woman ask Jesus: "Are you greater than our father Jacob?"

[173] See John 1:45 (cf. Matt 11:13 and Luke 24:44); 8:53; 12:41 (Isaiah saw Jesus' glory and spoke of him). In b. Sanh. 99a (Soncino 670) it is stated that "all the prophets prophesied only in respect to the Messianic era."

[174] See John 11, the raising of Lazarus, who had been dead for four days (v. 17), and 1 Kgs. 17:17-24 (2 Kgs. 4:18-37 similarly of Elisha).

[175] See John 6:1-15, the feeding of the 5000 with five barley loaves and two fish. In 2 Kgs. 4:42-44, Elisha's twenty loaves of barley and fresh ears of grain feed only 100 men.

[176] John 1:8, 15, 19-24, 26-35; 3:28-30; 4:1.

The Fourth Evangelist would not emphasize the motif of Jesus' "being more than" all these scriptural figures, plus John the Baptist, if he did not want to address people for whom they were very important. By means of this theme, he seeks to win over his fellow Jews to belief in Jesus as the expected Messiah, who is greater than them all.

Rabbinic traditions may have aided him in these comparisons. In addition to the contrast to Ahasuerus above, it should be noted that in Exod. Rab. Beshallach 25/8 on Exod 16:4 ("bread from heaven"), God in the time-to-come will ask someone at the messianic banquet to say grace. After Michael, Gabriel, the patriarchs, Moses, Aaron, and the elders defer, David is given the honor, for a king should bless a King.[177] In b. Pes. 119b grace is said after this "great banquet," and the order is Abraham, Isaac, Jacob, Moses, Joshua, and David.[178]

Another strand of tradition interprets the "great mountain" of Zech 4:7 as the King Messiah, who is greater than the patriarchs, more exalted than Moses, and higher than the angels of service.[179] Finally, Midr. Ps. 18/29 on Ps 18:38 relates that in the time-to-come God will seat the King Messiah at his right hand (the place of honor), as Ps 110:1 is interpreted. When He seats Abraham at his left, the latter's face "turns pale."[180]

Although these rabbinic traditions are now found in late sources, they certainly reflect earlier Judaic thought about the Messiah: he will be greater than the angels, the patriarchs and Moses. The Fourth Evangelist also emphasizes the same theme, in addition favorably comparing Jesus to Ahasuerus in 2:1-11.

VI. DIONYSOS AND THE CHANGING OF WATER INTO WINE

While the Fourth Evangelist is definitely a Jewish Christian, he aims his gospel not only at Jews, but also at non-Jews. For example, he translates Hebrew and Aramaic terms for them into Greek.[181] He is also the only evangelist to mention that some Greeks had also gone to worship in Jerusalem

---

[177]Soncino 3.310.

[178]Soncino 616.

[179]See Tanchuma B Toledoth 20 in S. Buber, *Midrasch Tanchuma* (Vilna: Romm, 1885) 139. A German translation is found in H. Bietenhard, *Midrasch Tanhuma B* (Bern: Peter Lang, 1980) 1.149. See also Tanchuma Toledoth 14; Targ. Neb. and Yalqut Shim'oni on Zech 4:7; as well as Pesiq. R. 37/1 (Braude 2.685), where the patriarchs acknowledge that the Messiah is greater than they because he has suffered for their children. On the latter motif, cf. n. 2 in Braude.

[180]See Buber, *Midrasch Tehillim* 157, and Braude, *The Midrash on Psalms* 1.261. Abraham's face "turning pale" (כָּרְבַּס) before the Messiah recalls Ahasuerus' goblets "changing" before the Temple vessels. As noted above, that imagery is based on King Belshazzar's face "changing" in the book of Daniel.

[181]See John 1:38,41,42; 4:25; 9:7; 19:17; 20:16. Again, I do not raise the possibility of a later redactor here.

at the feast of Passover (12:20), and to note the theme of teaching the Greeks in the dispersion (7:35).

To impress possible Jewish converts, the Fourth Evangelist employed the theme described above of Jesus' "being more than" the most important figures in Judaism. To impress possible non-Jewish converts, he himself may have also intended a contrast between Jesus' turning water into wine at Cana, and Dionysos, the wine god.

Over a century ago P. Cassel in his special study of John 2:1-11 drew attention to Hellenistic sources dealing with the miraculous flow of wine at the festival of this Greek god.[182] Without referring to him, R. Bultmann later proposed that the Dionysos legend was the origin of the miracle.[183]

In light of the material adduced above from Judaic haggadah on Esther 1, Bultmann's theory can no longer be maintained; nor is a modification of it valid as proposed by E. Linnemann. She maintains the narrative arose in a Christian congregation which had to present its case for Jesus vis-à-vis a group which practiced the mystery cult of Dionysos.[184]

Yet Greek-speaking non-Jews would almost automatically have compared Jesus as represented in John 2:1-11 with Dionysos. His cult was practiced from India to Ethiopia, to Italy, but especially in Asia Minor.[185]

Writing in the middle of the first century B.C.E., Diodorus Siculus notes that many Greek cities claimed to be the wine god's place of birth. "The Teans advance as proof *(tekmērion,* 'a sure sign') that the god was born among them the fact that, even to this day, at fixed times (the festival of Dionysos) in their city a fountain of wine, of unusually sweet fragrance, flows of its own accord *(automatōs)* from the earth."[186] He continues by saying: "the god has left behind him in many places over the inhabited world evidences *(sēmeia)* of his personal favor and presence."[187]

This "miracle," as M. Nilsson correctly describes it, is designed to prove the annual or at least regular epiphany, or appearance, of Dionysos. It is a sign or proof/evidence that he is present. Wine also gushed forth from fountains in other localities associated with Dionysos.[188]

---

[182]*Die Hochzeit von Cana* 138-39.

[183]*Das Evangelium des Johannes* 83, especially n. 3.

[184]"Die Hochzeit zu Kana und Dionysos" in *NTS* 20 (1974) 408-18, especially 418.

[185]See H. Noetzel, *Christus und Dionysos* (Stuttgart: Calwer, 1960) 17-25.

[186]Book III. 66,1-2 in the LCL translation of C.H. Oldfather. For the dating, see LCL 1.ix.

[187]See 66,3.

[188]See Nilsson's *Geschichte der griechischen Religion* (Munich: Beck, 1955[2]) I.585-90, especially the last two pages, for these localities.

The example most relevant to John 2:1-11, however, is the following. At the end of the second century C.E. Pausanias wrote his *Description of Greece,* in which he recorded the worship of Dionysos at Elis near Olympia on the Peloponnesus. He stated regarding this festival:

> Three pots (*lebētas*) are brought into the building by the priests and set empty in the presence of the citizens and of any strangers who may chance to be in the country. The doors of the building are sealed by the priests themselves and by any others who may be so inclined. On the morrow they are allowed to examine the seals, and on going into the building they find the pots filled with wine.... The Andrians too assert that every other year at their feast of Dionysos wine flows of its own accord (*automaton*) from the sanctuary.[189]

The mechanical device by which the priests secretly filled wine into these pots has been described by Heron the Alexandrian.[190] It is probable that a similar religious fraud took place in Temple B in nearby Corinth, dating from the fifth century B.C.E.[191]

The Olympic Games took place directly next to Elis until the end of the fourth century C.E. Since a pre-first century C.E. date seems probable for the mechanism at Corinth mentioned above,[192] I also consider it probable that Pausanias' description of the Elis wine miracle or epiphany basically also applied to the first century C.E. If this is so, knowledge of it would have spread throughout the Greek-speaking world via athletes and spectators at the Olympian Games.[193]

The above Dionysos material may have had consequences for John 2:1-11. The Fourth Evangelist could have changed the phrase in his source, "showed his glory" in v. 11, to "*manifested* his glory" precisely in order to compete with the wine god Dionysos known to him and his readers. Streams, from which water up till then had flowed, were thought to gush with wine at the god's epiphany or "manifestation."

---

[189]Book VI, 26.1-2 in the LCL translation of W.H. Jones. On the dating, see LCL 1.ix. There are parallel traditions in (Pseudo-) Aristotle, Mirabilia 123 (Aristotelis Opera, II Volumen Alterum, ed. I. Bekker; Berlin: de Gruyter, 1960, p. 842) and Athenaei Naueratitae, *Dipnosophistarum* Book XV, 34a (ed. G. Kaibel; Leipzig: Teubner, 1887, p. 78). They both note that the kettles are of copper.

[190]See Nilsson, *Geschichte* I 590, notes 4-5.

[191]See C. Bonner, "A Dionysiac Miracle at Corinth," in the *American Journal of Archaeology* 33 (1929) 368-75.

[192]See n. 191.

[193]The inhabitants of Elis, for example, honored Herod the Great for his financial support of the Olympic Games. Hellenized Jews from Palestine may have attended the Games as spectators and also related at home their accounts of events in the vicinity. See A. Schalit, *König Herodes. Der Mann und sein Werk* (Studia Judaica 4; Berlin: de Gruyter, 1969) 417.

Secondly, the Fourth Evangelist may also have changed the number of water jars for purification standing in the wedding house of his source into six. Perhaps his source had "many," or four or five in order to emphasize the superabundance of the water turned into wine by Jesus. The number six, however, definitely does not refer to the wine preserved by God for the righteous since the "six" days of creation.[194] It may, however, be the Evangelist's attempt to say: At Jesus' epiphany we experience more, even *twice* as much as in the Dionysos epiphany miracle (three). Jesus supersedes not only Ahasuerus and the venerated figures of Judaism, but also the most popular pagan god. He is greater than them all. He is the Messiah, the Son of God. From his fulness *all* have received, both Jew and Greek.

---

[194]Noetzel, *Christus und Dionysos* 46.

Part Two

HEROD ANTIPAS' BIRTHDAY BANQUET IN MARK 6:17-29, AND AHASUERUS' BIRTHDAY BANQUET IN JUDAIC TRADITIONS ON ESTHER 1

The wedding feast at Cana in John 2:1-11 is not the only narrative in the NT which is dependent on Judaic traditions regarding Ahasuerus' banquet(s) in Esther 1. The story of Herod Antipas' birthday banquet, involving the beheading of John the Baptist in Mark 6:17-29 (see also Matt 14:1-12 and Luke 3:19-20; 9:7-9), also betrays knowledge of the same complex of traditions.

Because the portrayal of the Baptist's end is so colorful and its dramatic tension is high, it has been very popular throughout the centuries, including presentation not only in paintings, but also in the 1905 opera "Salome" by Richard Strauss. This in turn was based on Oscar Wilde's 1893 literary work of the same name. Yet the very popularity of the gruesome episode of John's beheading has tended to restrain thorough analysis of it. Perhaps there has been some unconscious fear of ruining a "work of art" by dissecting it into its original parts. In the following, I shall do the latter. I hope, however, the analysis will lead to an even greater appreciation of the author's (or pl.) narrative ability, and of the great theological significance of the account in its present context.

It has long been observed that there seems to be a Semitic background to Mark 6:17-29. J. Wellhausen in 1903 pointed out the *autos* of v. 17 and the *autēs* of v. 22 as Aramaisms,[1] and other scholars believe they can recognize

---

[1]Cf. his *Das Evangelium Marci* (Berlin: Reimer, 1903) 48. For recent secondary literature on the Baptist narrative, see H.M. Humphrey, *A Bibliography for the Gospel of Mark 1954-1980* (Studies in the Bible and Early Christianity, 1; New York and Toronto: Mellen, 1981) 69.

more.[2] Building on Wellhausen's observation that the phrase *synetērei auton* in v. 20 (Herod Antipas "kept him [John] safe") corresponds to the Aramaic נְטַר,[3] I suggest that there was additional wordplay with the root נטר in the original Aramaic version of the narrative.

The preceding verse (19) states that Herodias "had a grudge against" John. The Greek verb employed here, *enechō* with the dative, is found in the gospels only here and in Luke 11:53. The only occurrence of this verb in the LXX with a Hebrew equivalent is Gen 49:23, where the MT has שָׂטַם. Yet in rabbinic Hebrew and Aramaic נְטַר/נָטַר especially means "to reserve anger," "to bear a grudge against," as the well-known verse Lev 19:18 attests.[4] Herod Antipas is thought of as "preserving" John, yet his new wife Herodias "bore a grudge against" the Baptist. The same Semitic root is employed for both phrases.

Finally, Mark 6:17 describes Herod Antipas as binding John in "prison" *(phylakē)*, a term which is repeated in v. 27. This can be expressed by בֵּית מַטְּרָא, מַט׳, מַטַּרְתָּא, also from the same root as above.[5]

In other words, the Judaic liking for wordplays found so frequently in the targums, talmuds, and midrashim, is also apparent in vv. 17, 19, 20 and 27 here. This corroborates the Semitic background proposed by others for the pericope, and supports the case I shall now make for at least ten ways in which the narrative of the beheading of John is dependent on Hebrew and Aramaic Judaic haggadic traditions on Esther, primarily chapter 1. Later, when the original Aramaic narrative was translated into Greek, terminology from the same biblical source (LXX Esther) was logically also employed. The background of the Baptist narrative in the Scroll of Esther was also recognized by the Greek translator(s).

Following that presentation (Section VII), I shall discuss the original language, literary form, content and origin of the Baptist narrative (Section VIII), its significance in the present Marcan context (Section IX), and finally, by means of delimitation, what the narrative is not (Section X).

---

[2] See the convenient summary in H. Hoehner, *Herod Antipas* (Cambridge: Cambridge University, 1972) 118, n. 3. His chapter seven is entitled "Antipas and John the Baptist," pp. 110-71.

[3] *Das Evangelium Marci* 48. On the Hebrew נְטַר, Aramaic נְטַר, נְטִיר, see Jastrow 901: to guard, observe, reserve, preserve. See also BDB 643 and 1102. On *syntēreō* in the sense of "preserve," see LXX Dan 3:23, of the three men cast into the furnace.

[4] Jastrow 901. For a tannaitic explanation of "bearing a grudge," see b. Yoma 23a (Soncino English 103-04). The related noun employed there, נְטִירָה, especially means "bearing a grudge" (Jastrow 899).

[5] Jastrow 770. The same root is found in 1 Targ Est 2:21 (the מַנְטוֹרֵי, "guardians" of the palace; Grossfeld 13) and the second targum ("keepers," מָנְטְרֵי, of the wardrobe; Cassel Aramaic 40), and 1 Targ Est 6:2 (מַנְטוֹרֵי, Grossfeld 25) and the second targum ("guardians," נָטְרֵי, of the king's head; Cassel Aramaic 59).

VII.   AFFINITIES OF MARK 6:17-29 WITH BIBLICAL AND JUDAIC TRADITIONS ON ESTHER, ESPECIALLY CHAPTER 1

A.   Herod Antipas Called a "King"

While his father Herod the Great (reigned 37-4 B.C.E.) bore the title "king," as did the brother of his second wife Herodias, Herod Agrippa I, as of 37 C.E.,[6] Herod Antipas never did. From 4 B.C.E. to 39 C.E. he was merely "tetrarch" of Galilee and Perea, the latter a territory east of the Jordan River, to the southeast of Galilee.[7] Although Matthew retained the term "king" for Antipas at 14:9, in his adaptation of the Marcan narrative he intentionally omitted all the other "king" references and correctly spoke of "Herod the tetrarch" in 14:1. Luke's designation of Herod in 3:19 and 9:7 is similarly correct historically.

In his own gospel Mark employs the term "king" a total of twelve times, of which almost half occur in the larger narrative of Herod Antipas' birthday banquet (6:14,22,25,26,27). In addition, the term "kingdom" is found in v. 23. This phenomenon alone would indicate the basically non-Marcan origin of 6:17-29. Elsewhere the evangelist is much more sparing in his use of this title.

Hoehner suggests that the designation of Herod Antipas as "king" is either due to "the popular terminology of the day," or to "courtesy."[8] However, it is best explained by the narrative's dependence on the Scroll of Esther. In no other biblical book does this title occur so frequently: מֶלֶךְ of King Ahasuerus 136 times in the Hebrew, *basileus* of the Persian ruler 157 times in the LXX, including the "additions" to Esther. In the first chapter of the Hebrew Esther alone, Ahasuerus is labeled "king" twenty times, including vv. 2-3. The latter are decisive for "King" Herod Antipas' banquet, as I propose in Section VII, C below.

The impression the present reader gets when reading Mark 6:21 is that Antipas' banquet took place in Galilee. Unless one had some previous information, one would have no reason to think of the far-off Perean fortress of Machaerus near the Dead Sea, where according to Josephus the tetrarch imprisoned and had John killed.[9] If so, the site of the banquet, at least in the

---

[6]On the latter, see Philo, *In Flaccum* 40, as well as Josephus, *Ant.* 19.328. For the dating of both, see E. Schürer, *The History of the Jewish People in the Age of Jesus Christ (175 B.C. - A.D. 135)*, ed. G. Vermes and F. Millar (Edinburgh: Clark, 1973) 1.287 and 444, respectively.

[7]Schürer, *The History* 1.341.

[8]*Herod Antipas* 150.

[9]*Ant.* 18.119. It has been estimated that the distance between Machaerus and Tiberias on the Sea of Galilee was at least four days of travel in one direction.

present Marcan setting, was Tiberias, which Herod Antipas had made his new capital, founding it perhaps ca. 23 C.E.[10]

In the light of the above information Est 1:2-3 appears even more probable as the background for Mark 6:21, especially the very strong Marcan emphasis on Herod as "king." The Esther verses state that "King" Ahasuerus in his "capital" also gave a "banquet" for all his government and military officials.

I shall comment in detail in Section VII, D on the latter groups of people. Here it suffices to note that the historically false and unusually frequent designation of Herod Antipas as "king" in Mark 6:17-29 can very well be due to dependence on the original narrator's prototype, Esther 1.

B. The King's Perplexity

Mark 6:20 states regarding "King" Herod Antipas and John: "And having heard him, he was much perplexed, and he heard him gladly." The commentators themselves are perplexed at this verse. F. Grant, for example, maintains: "Something has gone wrong with the text at this point...."[11]

The second half of v. 20 makes better sense if one interprets the Greek *kai*, literally "and," as "and yet," "nevertheless."[12] The influence of the Semitic "waw" as "but" shows through here, which the Greek translator too simply rendered as "and."[13]

The major problem, however, lies in the phrase "he was much perplexed," in Greek *polla ēporei*. The basic form of the verb is *aporeō*. In its other five occurrences in the NT, the middle form is employed: *aporeomai*. It means to be at a loss, in doubt, puzzled, perplexed.[14] Philo, for example, states in *Mos.* 2.217 that, like Herod Antipas, Moses was "perplexed" as to what should be done to someone put into prison.[15] 1 Macc 3:31 employs a phrase similar to the Marcan one: King Antiochus was "greatly perplexed" in his mind (*ēporeito...sphodra*). The latter term is better Greek than the Marcan *polla*.

Matthew at 14:5 omitted Herod Antipas' perplexity when he retold the Baptist narrative, perhaps also sensing the same question that the modern reader

---

This would make the participation of the Galileans mentioned in 6:21 improbable. See A. Merx, *Das Evangelium Matthaeus* (Berlin: Reimer, 1902) 229, n. 2.

[10]Hoehner, *Herod Antipas* 93-95. Cf. also Schürer, *The History* 2.179 for 17-20 C.E. Tiberias is mentioned in the NT only in connection with the "Sea of Tiberias" (John 6:1 and 21:1), and with boats from the city (6:23).

[11]"The Gospel According to St. Mark," in *Interpreter's Bible* 7 (1951) 735.

[12]BAGD 392, 2.g.

[13]BDB 252, 1.e; Jastrow 371.

[14]BAGD 97; LSJ 214. The noun *aporia*, occurring in Luke 21:25, can also mean perplexity.

[15]See also 2:165; *Leg. Gai.* 263 regarding Herod Agrippa I; and Josephus, *Bell.* 1.310 regarding Herod the Great.

poses: "Why should the king have been perplexed at all?" There seems to be no real reason for this puzzlement. Understandably, one commentator believes the phrase is misplaced, deriving from 6:16. Another thinks it is a gloss.[16] Others prefer the much less attested reading *polla epoiei*, meaning here "he did it much," that is, "he heard him often."[17]

There is, however, good reason for retaining the best attested form *polla ēporei* found in the Nestle-Aland NT. This puzzling phrase also derives from Judaic haggadic comment on King Ahasuerus' banquet scene in Esther 1.

Before the Persian king has his queen, Vashti, killed and her head is brought to him on a platter (see Section VII, 1.2), Ahasuerus is portrayed as dining at his (birthday) banquet, and he is merry with wine (1:10). He then orders his seven eunuchs to bring Vashti before him. The name of the first of these is Mehuman, מְהוּמָן.

Judaic commentators could not resist a play on this word. They also maintained that the "king" who spoke in 1:10 was not Ahasuerus, but God (the "King of Kings"). Midrash Abba Gorion on this verse, for example, states: "'He (the King) spoke to Mehuman.' This is the angel appointed over confusion (מְהוּמָה)."[18] Leqach Tob on this verse also reads מְהוּמָה.[19] Aggadat Esther on

---

[16]See for the first, Schmiedel, quoted in Grant, "The Gospel According to St. Mark," 735. For the second, Grant refers to E. Klostermann, *Das Markusevangelium* (HNT, 3; Tübingen: Mohr, 1950[4]) 59: "this almost appears to be a gloss."

[17]This is not the more "difficult" reading, as maintained by Kostermann, *ibid.*, and E. Lohmeyer, *Das Evangelium des Markus* (Meyer 1,2; Göttingen: Vandenhoeck & Ruprecht, 1963) 119, n. 5. Lack of comprehension as to why the king was perplexed at all led to the minor changes of the *ē* to *e,* and the substitution of *i* for *r* in *ēporei.* The poorer reading is followed by F. Delitzsch in *Ha-Berit ha-chadashah* (London: British and Foreign Bible Society, 1958) 72, as well as *Sifre ha-Berit ha-chadashah* (Jerusalem: United Bible Societies, 1979) 105. The Hebrew could be נָבוֹךְ מְאֹד (see n. 25), less probably הָמַם.

[18]For the noun see Jastrow 737. It is related to the verb הָמַם, "to confuse" (BDB 243). A German translation is offered in A. Wünsche, *Aus Israels Lehrhallen* (Leipzig, 1907; reprint Hildesheim: Olms, 1967) 2.104. Wünsche employs the text of A. Jellinek, *Bet ha-Midrasch* (Leipzig, 1877; reprinted Jerusalem: Wahrmann, 1967) I, p. 3. He correctly prefers it to Buber, *Aggadic Books* 14, who has חֵימָה, "wrath," in his text, but מְהוּמָה as a variant in his n. 202. The haggadic tradition is from R. Yochanan (bar Nappacha), a second generation Palestinian Amora (Strack and Stemberger, *Einleitung* 91). For this reason I consider the word חֵימָה in Est. Rab. 3/12 on Est 1:10, also in R. Yochanan's name, to be a corruption. See Lewin-Epstein 13a, and Soncino 9.53. The original probably had "confusion and wrath," as in Aggadat Esther (see the following).

[19]Buber, *Aggadic Books* 92.

1:10 is fuller: "'Mehuman': This is the angel appointed over confusion (מְהוּמָה) and over wrath (חֵמָה)."[20]

The first targum on Est 1:10 strongly emphasizes this confusion/perplexity. Because of Mordecai's extensive fasting since the beginning of the royal feasts,[21] his cry and that of the Sanhedrin in Susa came before the Lord. In order to "confound" (לערבלא)[22] the king's feast, the Lord "incited against him the angel of 'confusion' (שְׁגּוּשְׁתָּא)...."[23] Mehuman was appointed over מְהוּמְתָּא, "confusion, perplexity."[24] The Lord will also "confound" (לצדאותהון)[25] all the seven princes who serve King Ahasuerus.

The targum here combines views of the seven princes as angels, as in Abba Gorion, and as the mortal victims of God's punishment. These views stand side by side, pointing to several earlier traditions. What is important to note, however, is that the targum not only includes the wordplay of Mehuman and מְהוּמָה, "confusion, perplexity," but also three other Aramaic terms for this emotional state. I suggest that because of the great emphasis on this motif here, the Aramaic writer of the Baptist narrative noted in Mark 6:20 that "King" Herod Antipas was "greatly perplexed." For him, this corresponded to God's inciting against King Ahasuerus the angel of confusion/perplexity.

Only after this perplexity of King Ahasuerus in Judaic tradition does the monarch give the order to have Queen Vashti's head cut off. The same sequence is also found in Mark 6: first "King" Herod Antipas is perplexed, then he orders John to be decapitated.

---

[20]S. Buber, *Aggadath Esther* (Cracow, 1897; reprinted with additions in Israel, 1963-64) 13.

[21]The targum does not state the reason for the fasting at this point. However, in its comment on 1:5 it notes that the Israelites who did partake of the banquet were sinners. See Grossfeld 6 and 41, and other rabbinic sources cited in his n. 13 on pp. 80-81. In Est. Rab. 7/13 on Est 3:9 (Soncino 9.97), R. Ishmael (ben Elisha, a second-generation Tanna: Strack and Stemberger, *Einleitung* 97) says regarding 1:5 that the 18,500 Israelites who went to Ahasuerus' banquet hall ate, drank, became drunk and "disgraced themselves with immorality" (the nithpa. of קִלְקֵל is employed here: Jastrow 1382; Lewin-Epstein 23a). This accords with the view expressed before this, that harlots were present.

[22]Jastrow 1113 on עַרְבֵּל.

[23]*Ibid.*, 1558: "confusion, perplexity, excitement."

[24]*Ibid.*, 737.

[25]*Ibid.*, 1262, צְדִי. For the Aramaic text of Est 1:10, see Grossfeld 7; the English is on p. 42. The first targum on Est 3:15 also notes that the city of Susa was "perplexed" (Grossfeld 19 and 55), commenting on the Hebrew word בּוּךְ, "to perplex, confuse" (BDB 100). At 6:1, as an explanation of the king's inability to fall asleep, the same targum speaks of the Lord's commanding "the angel who was in charge of disturbance (שִׁיגּוּשְׁתָּא) to descend and disturb (שַׁגֵּישׁ) Ahasuerus" (Grossfeld 25 and 61). This tradition is also found in the second targum here (Cassel Aramaic 59).

C. The Birthday Banquet

Mark 6:21 states that Herod Antipas made a "banquet" *(deipnon)* on the occasion of his own "birthday" *(ta genesia)*. Both of these motifs also derive from Judaic haggadic traditions regarding Esther 1.

1. The Banquet

Est 1:3 has King Ahasuerus in his capital give a "banquet." This is מִשְׁתֶּה in the MT and *doche* in the LXX, which has another Greek term, *potos*, at vv. 5, 8 and 9. The "A" text of the LXX has *potos* in vv. 3 and 5, *doche* in v. 9, and *symposion* in v. 11.[26] Josephus in *Ant.* 11.186 speaks at this point of a lavish "feast," *heistia*, and in 187 of a *symposion*.

Although none of the above sources employs *deipnon* for מִשְׁתֶּה, the four different Greek terms which translate the same Hebrew word that the Marcan synonym *deipnon* could also be used. It was a frequent term for "banquet" in NT times.[27]

2. Herod Antipas' Birthday

The term *ta genesia* only occurs in the NT in Mark 6:21 and the parallel, Matt 14:6. Nor is it found in the LXX.[28] The rareness of the word suggests that in Mark it may derive from a post-biblical source.

It is known that the Jews of Rome celebrated the birthday of Herod Antipas' father, Herod the Great, as a holiday.[29] In *Ant.* 19.321 Josephus relates that the brother of Herodias, Agrippa I, later celebrated his birthday with joyous festivities for all his subjects. The portrayal of Herod Antipas as having a large birthday banquet thus fits the Herodian family well, even if he was only tetrarch of Galilee and Perea and not "king" like them.

The Mishna at Abodah Zarah 1:3 mentions the "day of גְּנוּסְיָא of (pagan) kings" as a festival.[30] This day is not the annual anniversary of a king's accession to power,[31] but his birthday, as the Palestinian Talmud correctly notes

---

[26]Clines, *The Esther Scroll* 218-21.

[27]Cf. the article *deipnon, deipneō* by J. Behm in *TDNT* 2.34-35. Luke 14:12-13 interchanges *deipnon* with *ariston* and *doche*.

[28]The term *genethlios* is found in 2 Macc 6:7 as well as in the "D" text of Mark 6:21.

[29]See Persius Flaccus, *The Satires* 5.180, in the Latin and English edition of J. Jenkinson (Wiltshire: Aris & Phillips, 1980) 52: *Herodis...dies*. He notes on p. 1 that Persius was active between 34-62 C.E. Lohmeyer called attention to this passage in his *Das Evangelium des Markus,* Ergänzungsheft 11.

[30]Ch. Albeck, *The Six Orders of the Mishnah* (Hebrew; Jerusalem - Bialik, Tel Aviv - Dvir, 1975) 4.325. For the term, cf. Jastrow 240, as well as Krauss, *Lehnwörter* 2.180.

[31]So interpreted in b. Abodah Zarah 10a (Soncino 49-50), which Danby follows in *The Mishnah* 437.

in 39c at this point.[32] It appropriately quotes Gen 40:20, where on his "birthday" Pharaoh also made a feast for all his servants, which involved the hanging of the chief baker (v. 22). In *De Ios.* 97-98 Philo describes this episode by stating that when the king's birthday *(genethlios)* arrived, "all the inhabitants of the country held festive gatherings, and particularly those of the palace." When the officials were banqueting, the king ordered (the chief baker, up to then imprisoned) to be impaled and his head cut off *(apotemnō).*[33]

This biblical combination of a king's birthday banquet and a prisoner's being decapitated influenced Judaic haggadic traditions on Esther 1, in which Queen Vashti's head is cut off and put on a platter. While I shall comment on the decapitation of John in Section VII, I, at this point rabbinic sources may be cited which state that King Ahasuerus' banquet in his capital in Est 1:3 was not on the occasion of his wedding to Vashti, as stressed in the above essay on John 2, nor for several other reasons. Rather, it was his birthday: יוֹם גְּנוּסְיָא. This is mentioned in the midrashim Abba Gorion, Panim Achérim B, Leqach Tob[34] and Aggadat Esther,[35] as well as Yalqut Shim'oni § 1047, all on Est 1:3.[36]

D. The Guests

Mark 6:21 relates that Herod Antipas gave a banquet on his birthday "for his nobles and the chiliarchs and the leading men" of Galilee: *tois megistasin autou kai tois chiliarchois kai tois prōtois.*

It has been estimated that the city of Tiberias, newly built by Herod Antipas, had a population of between thirty and forty thousand.[37] At the beginning of the war with Rome, from 66-70 C.E., it had a council of 600 members.[38] Ten "first men" *(prōtoi)* were at the head of this council.[39] The

---

[32]English in J. Neusner, *The Talmud of the Land of Israel,* 33: *Abodah Zarah* (Chicago: University of Chicago, 1982) 24. See also Schürer, *The History* 1. 346-48.

[33]Cf. the English translation of F. Colson in the LCL edition of Philo, as well as 96.

[34]Buber, *Aggadic Books* 8, 58 and 89, respectively.

[35]Buber, *Aggadath Esther* 10.

[36]See also the variant reading of the first targum to Est 1:3 (Grossfeld 193: the king had an עִדְיָא, an anniversary), as well as Haman's complaint to King Ahasuerus regarding the Jews in the same targum on 3:8: "Our birthdays they do not celebrate" (Grossfeld 18 and 54). This implies that the King does celebrate his own. In the fourth century B.C.E., Plato, after referring to Artaxerxes and Xerxes, noted regarding the Persian king: "The whole of Asia celebrates the king's birthday with sacrifices and feasting." See Alcibiades I 121c in the LCL translation of W. Lamb, pp. 166-67.

[37]M. Avi-Yonah, cited by Hoehner, *Herod Antipas* 97.

[38]Josephus, *Bell.* 2.641. Cf. other references in Hoehner, *Herod Antipas* 97, n. 7.

[39]Josephus, *Vita* 69 and 296. Different words are used for the same term in 168 and *Bell.* 2.639. Cf. also the *prōtoi* of the city in *Vita* 64 and 67.

latter term may have partly influenced the selection of *hoi prōtoi* in Mark 6:21, if this council was known to the Greek translator(s) of 6:17-29.

Yet again, the main model for the entire phrase in Mark 6:21 is Est 1:3, as was true for Sections VII, A and VII, C above. There King Ahasuerus makes a banquet in his capital for a) "all his princes (שָׂרָיו) and servants, b) the army (חֵיל) of Persia and Media, and c) the nobles (פַּרְתְּמִים) and princes (שָׂרֵי) of the provinces before him."

a) In the LXX, *hoi megistanes* translates שָׂרִים eight times,[40] showing that in the Semitic original of the beheading of John the Baptist, שָׂרִים or its Aramaic equivalent most probably was employed. Following the LXX, this term was later logically translated into Greek as *hoi megistanes*.

b) Leaving out the servants as irrelevant, the narrator knew of the tradition still found in the first targum's translation of the general word "army" of Est 1:3 as "troops/armies" (אוֹכְלוֹסֵי)[41] of Persia and Media, "generals" (אִיסְטְרַטֵיגִין)[42] and "chiefs" (רַבְנִין) appointed over the provinces. In the Semitic original of Mark 6:21 the term "generals" was probably employed, as in the first targum. When the narrative was translated into Greek, the term "tribune" (*chiliarchos*) was chosen. It suited the nomenclature of Herod Antipas' own Jewish "troops," which was based on that of the Roman occupational power's army.[43] John 18:12 and Acts 21-24, for example, mention a Jerusalem "tribune," and Acts 25:23 notes the "tribunes and prominent men" of Caesarea in connection with a visit of King Agrippa II. Herod Antipas, only a tetrarch, probably had no "tribunes."[44] Yet neither was he a king. The narrator and/or the Greek translator exaggerate for effect.

---

[40]Cf. also the *megistanes* of Media and Persia at Darius' large banquet in 1 Esdr 3:1. See also 3:14 and *Ant.* 11.37.

[41]Jastrow 25.

[42]Jastrow 92 under אִסְטְרַטִיגוֹס. The term derives from the Greek *stratēgos*, "military commander," "general." Strangely, Grossfeld omits this word in his English translation (6 and 40). In the "A" version of LXX Est 1:11, Ahasuerus' banquet is also "before his army" (*stratia*). See Clines 220-21.

[43]See, for example, the Latin loan word *rufulus* ("military tribune," Jastrow 1463 on רוּפִילָא) in 1 Targ. Est 9:6 and 12 regarding army commanders in Susa (Grossfeld 32-33 and 68-69). Another factor involved may have been the frequent translation in the LXX of שַׂר אֶלֶף, "prince of a thousand," as *chiliarchos*. In the Hebrew New Testaments of Delitzsch and the United Bible Societies, *chiliarchoi* is translated by שָׂרֵי הָאֲלָפִים.

[44]S. Johnson in *A Commentary on the Gospel According to St. Mark* (Black's; London: Black, 1960) 120 writes: "The tetrarch was not allowed to keep an army, only a police force." For E. Haenchen the mention of chiliarchs to denote Herod Antipas' power is a "märchenhaft entstelltes Bild." See his *Der Weg Jesu. Eine Erklärung des Markus-Evangeliums und der kanonischen Quellen* (Berlin: de Gruyter, 1968[2]) 241.

c) Since the term for "nobles" in Est 1:3 is a Persian loan word,[45] it was irrelevant to the author of the Semitic original of Mark 6:21. He could, however, have made use of the next term, "princes" (שָׂרִים) of the provinces. The expression שָׂרִים in Est 2:18, where King Ahasuerus gives a large banquet for his "princes," is rendered by Josephus in *Ant.* 11.203 by *hoi prōtoi*. More importantly, the "princes" of Persia and Media who sit "first" in Ahasuerus' kingdom in Est 1:14 are called in the LXX *hoi prōtoi*. If the original narrator wrote in Aramaic, as I believe he did, the term רַבְנִין, "chiefs" of the provinces, as in 1 Targ. Est 1:3, could have been employed. A good Greek translation of the latter would also be *hoi prōtoi*, as in Mark 6:21. The "provinces" were simply changed to the singular province or tetrarchy of Galilee. Only the latter geographical area is mentioned in the gospel by name. If Herod Antipas' birthday banquet had taken place in Machaerus, where according to Josephus the tetrarch had John killed,[46] the additional phrase "and of Perea" would be necessary. This, too, points to the narrative of Mark 6:17-29 as being set in Tiberias, the capital (as in Est 1:3) of Galilee.

The RSV mentions "guests" at Herod Antipas' banquet in 6:22 and 26. The Greek is *hoi synanakeimenoi* and *hoi anakeimenoi*, respectively. Literally, the terms mean "to recline at table (with)."[47]   The only occurrence of *synanakeimenoi* in the LXX is in 3 Macc 5:39, where King Ptolemy's officials recline at table "with" him. Mark also has it at 2:15, which may indicate that he employed it in 6:22 to vary the style of the simpler form in v. 26.[48]

In his description of Ahasuerus' banquet(s) in Esther 1, Josephus relates that a pavilion was erected "so that myriads could recline at table" *(kataklinomai)*. He then calls the guests *hoi katakeimenoi (Ant.* 11.187-88), a synonym of *hoi anakeimenoi*. Josephus himself certainly did not "Romanize" the banquet of Ahasuerus by having the guests recline. He knew of this tradition from his source(s). Thus it is not surprising that Herod Antipas' birthday banquet guests also "recline at table" with him. In Judaic tradition, those of King Ahasuerus did precisely the same thing.

Finally, B. Weiss is certainly correct in his assertion that the guests are listed so extensively in Mark 6:21 in order to explain why Herod Antipas was then too embarrassed to say no to the girl (Herodias' daughter) before them.[49] He could not renege on his promise before so many important people.

---

[45]BDB 832.

[46]Cf. n. 9.

[47]See BAGD 784 and 55, respectively.

[48]Luke, who in general has a much better Greek, has the longer form at 7:49, 14:10 and 15.

[49]See his *Die vier Evangelien* (Leipzig: Hinrichs, 1905[2]) 1.208.

E. Salome as a "Little Girl"

The daughter of Herodias and Herod, the son of Herod the Great by Mariamme, was named Salome. She was first married to Herod the Great's son Philip, tetrarch of Trachonitis and other areas. The marriage was childless when he died in 33-34 C.E. She then married Aristobulus, by whom she had three sons.[50]

Salome's birth date is unknown, as is the duration of her marriage to Philip. If she had been married to him for several years, justifying Josephus' noting her childlessness, and if almost all Jewish girls were married at this time at the age of thirteen and one half to fourteen,[51] she may have been born ca. 16 C.E. The year of the beheading of John is also uncertain. Most commentators put it at the outset of Jesus' public ministry, ca. 28-29 C.E.[52] If so, Salome is pictured as being about twelve to thirteen years old in Mark 6.

In 6:22 and 28 (twice) she is called a *korasion*, a "little girl," the diminutive form of *korē*, "girl."[53] Mark employs the same term elsewhere only for Jesus' healing Jairus' "little girl" in 5:41-42. In v. 23 she is labeled a *thygatrion*, "little daughter"; in vv. 39-41 a *paidion*, "child"; and in v. 41 *talitha*, "girl."[54] The latter Aramaic term is explained for the Greek reader as a *korasion*, and in v. 42 it is noted that she was twelve years old.

Salome's behavior is depicted in the Marcan episode as that of an immature girl. By herself she would not have thought of leaving the women's quarters and dancing before well-mellowed men (6:22). That is, her mother Herodias stood behind her actions, as is shown in v. 24, where she exited to ask maternal advice in regard to what she should request. She immediately followed this advice (v. 25). Having received John's head on a platter, she did not retain it for herself, but gave it to her mother (v. 28), who had had a grudge against John and had wanted to kill him for some time (v. 19).

Such behavior to the modern mind would at the most warrant the term *korē*, "girl," but not *korasion*, "little girl." The latter, with the exception of the Marcan passages noted above, and their Matthean parallels, is not found

---

[50]*Ant.* 18.136-37, 106 and Schürer, *The History* 1.339-40.

[51]See the sources cited by Str-B 2.374-75. In *Ant.* 19.354 Bernice, the daughter of King Agrippa I, is mentioned as *already* married to her father's uncle, Herod, ruler of Chalcis, at the age of sixteen.

[52]Luke 3:19-20, 23; Mark 1:14. On this dating, cf. V. Taylor, *The Gospel According to St. Mark* (New York: St. Martin's, 1966[2]) 314, as well as R. Pesch, *Das Markusevangelium*, 1. Teil (Freiburg: Herder, 1984[4]) 342, n. 19: ca. 30 C.E. On problems with this chronology in the gospels and Josephus, see Wellhausen, *Das Evangelium Marci* 49, as well as W. Schenk, "Gefangenschaft und Tod des Täufers. Erwägungen zur Chronologie und ihren Konsequenzen" in *NTS* 29 (1983) 453-83.

[53]BAGD 444.

[54]On סַלְיְתָא, see Jastrow 537.

elsewhere in the NT, Philo, and Josephus. Again, the choice of this rare term derives from the Esther narrative.

Including variant readings, *korasion* occurs twenty-nine times in the LXX. Of these, eight are found in the Esther chapter directly following Ahasuerus' banquet: 2:2, 3, 7, 8, 9, 9AB, 12, 12A. Except for the last occurrence, the other seven all translate the Hebrew נַעֲרָה. In rabbinic Hebrew this is "a girl between twelve and twelve and a half years of age."[55] That is, as indicated above, a *korasion* for the Jewish translators of the LXX is of marriageable age.[56] For example, the *korasia* in Esther 2 hope to be chosen by King Ahasuerus as his new wife. 1 Kgs. 20:30 and Jdt. 16:12 even indicate that a *korasion* can already have a child or children.

The term "little girl" in the Baptist narrative, though strange to the modern mind, is thus appropriate to its context. Salome, probably herself about twelve or thirteen at this time, is a נַעֲרָה, a *korasion*. Yet she should not really be thought of as a "little" girl.

In the Semitic original of this narrative, נַעֲרָה would probably have been used if it was in Hebrew. If in Aramaic, as seems more probable, רְבִיתָא, "girl,"[57] could have been employed, as in 2 Targ. Est 2:12-13.[58] טַלְיְתָא, as in Mark 5:41, is also possible, occurring for example in 2 Targ. Est 2:9.[59]

F. The Dance of Death

Mark 6:22 has Salome, the daughter of Herodias, enter (from the adjacent women's chamber) and "dance" *(orcheomai)*[60] pleasingly before Herod Antipas and those reclining with him, i.e., the nobles, chiliarchs and leading men of Galilee who were attending his birthday banquet. The result is the gruesome death of John the Baptist.

Almost all the commentators agree that Salome's behavior here is hardly imaginable for a Herodian "princess." Whatever view one may have of this family's morals, no female member of the aristocracy would ever have performed a solo dance before a large group of half-drunk men. Examples of very chaste dancing by a female solo dancer in the previous or this century in Palestine are not to the point.[61] The question is rather of the Judaic attitude toward such dancing in the first century C.E. While there was dancing at weddings,

---

[55]Jastrow 922.

[56]See Tob 6:10 and 12.

[57]Jastrow 1443.

[58]Cassel Aramaic, 38-39.

[59]*Ibid.*, 38.

[60]The verb occurs in the NT only here, followed by Matthew in 14:6, and in the "Q" passage Matt 11:17 = Luke 7:32.

[61]Cf. G. Dalman, "Der Tanz der Tochter der Herodias" in *Palästinajahrbuch* 14 (1918) 44-46. One example he cites even takes place in Tiberias.

circumcisions, and large feasts, there is not a single example in early Judaism of the behavior attributed to Salome.[62] This motif must be sought elsewhere, in pagan customs.

It is known that non-Jews often had male or female dancers at their banquets or drinking bouts. Philo, for example, relates that the Roman Emperor Gaius (Caligula, reigning from 37-41 C.E.) could become "frantic with excitement at the sight of dancers," sometimes himself joining in the dance, or he would greet "a mime of scandalous scenes and broad jesting with a loud youngster's guffaw...."[63] Josephus also writes that once the Jew Joseph of Jerusalem went to Alexandria to marry his daughter to another high-ranking Jew. While there he dined with the Egyptian king, Ptolemy.[64] At this point a beautiful dancing-girl entered the banquet room, and Joseph immediately fell in love with her, although she was a "foreign woman," that is, a Gentile. Only Joseph's brother managed to save him from scandal by secretly substituting his own daughter for Joseph's amorous meetings with the girl, resulting in the man's marrying his own niece.[65]

Among the Greeks and Romans, female dancers who performed for men reclining at banquets or drinking bouts were courtesans or prostitutes.[66] The very negative Judaic attitude to such solo dancing is reflected in 2 Targ. Est 2:8. Hoping to be picked by the royal messengers to enter Ahasuerus' harem and possibly become the successor of Vashti, "the daughters of the heathen used to dance (מְרַקְדִין) and show their beauty through the windows...." The Jewish girl Esther, however, refused to deport herself so.[67]

Again, the immediate background of Salome's dancing, leading to the killing of John, is found in Judaic haggadic traditions on Ahasuerus' banqueting in Esther 1. Midrash Abba Gorion on Est 1:6, for example, states: "And there was pure purple under the feet of the attendants, and they danced (מְרַקְדִין) before those reclining."[68] Panim Achérim 2 on this verse says basically the same thing: "There was pure purple under the feet of the attendants, and they danced

---

[62]See the many sources cited in S. Krauss, *Talmudische Archäologie* (Leipzig: Fock, 1912) 3.99-102.

[63]*Leg. Gai.* 42, in the LCL translation of F. Colson. Directly before this a banquet is mentioned.

[64]Probably Ptolemy Epiphanes. Cf. n. "c" on *Ant.* 13.158 in the LCL edition. The time is ca. 200 B.C.E.

[65]*Ant.* 12.187-89.

[66]See F. Weege, *Der Tanz in der Antike* (Halle/Saale: Niemeyer, 1926), especially 118-24 on the Greeks (note illustration 175 on p. 124), and 153-55 on the Romans. Weege also deals with the Etruscans and Egyptians.

[67]Cassel English 301, Aramaic 38. Two parallels to this tradition are cited in Ginzberg, *The Legends* 6.458, n. 55.

[68]Buber, *Aggadic Books* 10. The Hebrew term employed here, מְסוּבָּה, literally means a reclining one, then guest. See Jastrow 804.

(הָיוּ פָרְקְדִין) on a pavement of precious stones and jewels before those reclining."[69]

Here the male attendants perform the dancing. In another haggadic tradition it is the wives of these banqueters who do so. To understand this, a Persian custom must first be cited.

In Herodotus 5.18 the Macedonian Amyntas prepares a magnificent banquet for the messengers of the Persian King Darius. After dinner the guests sit drinking with their host and state: "It is our Persian custom after the giving of any great banquet to bring in also the concubines and wedded wives to sit by the men."[70]

This Persian/Median usage is reflected in Pirq. R. El. 49, which relates regarding Est 1:8,10-12, and 19 the following:

> Rabbi Jose said: It was the universal custom of the kings of Media when they were eating and drinking to cause their women to come before them stark naked, playing and dancing (מְשַׂחֲקוֹת וּפָרְקְדוֹת), in order to see the beauty of their figures. When the wine entered the heart of Ahasuerus, he wished to act in this manner with Vashti the queen. She was the daughter of a king, and was not willing to do this. He decreed concerning her, and she was slain.[71]

The manner of Ahasuerus' having Vashti slain will be treated in Section VII, I. Here in Pirqe R. Eliezer on Esther 1 it is noteworthy that in contrast to the male dancers in the two haggadic traditions mentioned, female dancers, close relatives like Salome, are expected to perform at the king's banquet.

There is, however, another haggadic tradition which states that the dancing of only one person, like Salome, led to the execution of Vashti. In b. Meg. 11b on Est 1:2, Ahasuerus calculates how many of the seventy years prophesied for the desolation of Jerusalem in Jer 29:10 and Dan 9:2 have passed:[72]

---

[69]Buber, *op. cit.*, 59. This is also found in *Yalqut Shim'oni* § 1048 on Est. 1:6.

[70]Translation by A. Godley in the LCL edition. This seems to be reflected in Plutarch's Table-talk I.1, 613A, which P. Clement translates in the LCL edition of the *Moralia* VIII as: "They commend the Persians for doing their drinking and dancing with their mistresses rather than with their wives...." Est. Rab. 7/13 on Est 3:9 (Soncino 9.97) also states that at the banquet of 1:5 Ahasuerus had harlots.

[71]English in Friedlander, *Pirke de Rabbi Eliezer* 393-94, where the additional reading from the current editions is translated on p. 394, n. 2. For the Hebrew, see the Eshkol edition, 196. This scene is transferred in 2 Targ. Est 1:3 to King Solomon's banquet where, mellow with wine, he ordered all the creatures to perform a dance (לְמַרְקְדָא), which would show his guests his greatness. All came except the wood grouse, whom Solomon threatened to destroy. See the English in Cassel 276, the Aramaic in Cassel 13.

[72]See the first essay for this tradition.

When he saw that seventy had been completed and (the Jews) were not redeemed, he brought out the vessels of the Temple and used them. Then the Satan came and danced (רִיקֵד) among them and slew Vashti.[73]

Satan in rabbinic tradition is equated with the angel of death and the evil inclination.[74] The following passages attest this. In Gen. Rab. Noach 38/7 on Gen 11:2, R. Levi, a third-generation Palestinian Amora,[75] states: "Wherever you find eating and drinking, the dancer is up to mischief."[76] In Targ. Ps.-Jon. on Exod 32:19 Satan is among the (sinning) worshipers of the golden calf, dancing and leaping before the people.[77] Num. Rab. Balak 20/11 on Num 22:20 states that when someone is about to commit a sin, "Satan dances encouragingly before him until he completes the transgression," leading to his destruction.[78] Finally, the rabbis describe an ox which is liable to gore one to death by saying: "Satan is dancing between his horns."[79]

The above passages help to explain the statement in b. Meg. 11b that when Satan danced before Ahasuerus and his banquet guests, he slew Vashti. I suggest that this tradition from the haggadic development of Esther 1 stands behind Salome's dancing before "King" Herod Antipas and his guests at their own banquet. The result of that dancing was also the "king's" order to have someone slain: John the Baptist, as innocent as Vashti (see below).

G. Salome's "Pleasing" King Herod Antipas

Mark 6:22 relates that when Salome entered the banquet room, she "pleased" (areskō) King Herod Antipas and the men reclining at table with him. This motif of a korasion "pleasing" the king also derives from the Esther 1-2 complex.

After King Ahasuerus rid himself of his disobedient queen Vashti, his advisors suggested replacing her with a maiden who "pleases" the king. This

---

[73]Soncino 66.

[74]See b. B. Bat. 16a (Soncino 79).

[75]Strack and Stemberger, *Einleitung* 94.

[76]I have modified the Soncino translation in 1.307. I suggest because of the context that the Hebrew "arch-robber" (אַרְכִילִיסְטִיס, Greek *archilēstēs*) is here a corruption of the Greek for "dancer" (*orchēstēs*). The Hebrew of the latter is the very similar-sounding אַרְכֵיסְטִיס, no longer recognized by the copyist. He therefore substituted the better-known term "arch-robber." Two passages where the two terms are confused are cited by Krauss, *Lehnwörter* 2.131. For the passage, see J. Theodor and Ch. Albeck, *Midrash Bereshit Rabba* (Jerusalem: Wahrmann, 1965²) 1.356.

[77]English in Etheridge, *The Targums* 552; Aramaic in Rieder, *Targum Jonathan* 132. See also Pirq. R. El. 45 on the golden calf, where Satan is called Sammael (Friedlander 355).

[78]Soncino 6.797.

[79]Cf. b. Pes. 112b (Soncino 578) and b. Ber. 33a (Soncino 204).

search process, resulting in Esther's becoming the new queen, occupies all of Est 2:1-19, directly after the banquet scene of chapter one, so important for the background of the Baptist narrative.

The motif of "pleasing" the king is found in the following verses in the MT of Esther 2:

v. 4:   "And let the maiden who pleases (תִּיטַב בְּעֵינֵי)[80] the king be queen instead of Vashti."

v. 9:   "The maiden pleased (וַתִּיטַב ... בְּעֵינָיו) (Hegai, in charge of the women in the palace) and found his favor" (וַתִּשָּׂא חֶסֶד לְפָנָיו).

v. 14: "She did not go in to the king again, unless the king delighted in her (חָפֵץ בָּהּ) and she was summoned by name."

v. 15: "Esther found favor in the eyes of (נֹשֵׂאת חֵן בְּעֵינֵי) all who saw her."

v. 17: Esther "found grace and favor in (the king's) sight (וַתִּשָּׂא-חֵן וָחֶסֶד לְפָנָיו) more than all the virgins," so Ahasuerus made her the new queen.

This fivefold emphasis on "pleasing" the king is expressed in the targums primarily by שְׁפַר,[81] רְעֵי,[82] and סְעַן.[83] Especially noteworthy here is 2 Targ. Est 2:9: "And the girl pleased him." The Aramaic is: וּשְׁפֵירַת טַלְיְתָא בְעֵינוֹהִי.[84] The LXX renders this Hebrew verse as: kai ēpesen autō to korasion, employing the same two words as in Mark 6:22, areskō and korasion.[85]

The midrashim on the Scroll of Esther also emphasize the girl Esther's "pleasing" the king. One early example deals with her great beauty, which attracted Ahasuerus. It is found in Est. Rab. 6/9 on Est 2:15, where R. Judah (bar Ilai), a third-generation Tanna,[86] states: "She was like a statue which a thousand persons looked upon and all equally admire." R. Nehemiah, who frequently disputed with R. Judah,[87] then adds: "They put Median women on one side of her and Persian women on the other, and she was more beautiful than all of them."[88]

---

[80]From יטב, BDB 405: to be good, well, glad, "pleasing." Delitzsch (72) employs this verb in his Hebrew translation of Mark 6:22.
[81]Jastrow 1619.
[82]Ibid., 1486.
[83]Ibid., 544. For the first targum, see Grossfeld 10-13; for the second, Cassel Aramaic 36-39.
[84]Cassel Aramaic 38.
[85]In his retelling of this incident, Josephus in Ant. 11.202 (see also 196) employs the synonym hēdomai.
[86]Strack and Stemberger, Einleitung 83.
[87]Ibid.
[88]Soncino 9.77. See also b. Meg. 13a on Est 2:15 and 17 (Soncino 76-77).

The "A" text of the LXX, however, emphasizes not only Esther's beauty. It states on Est 2:17: "And when the king had examined (in bed) all the maidens, Esther proved the most outstanding." Indeed, whenever she was taken to the king, "she pleased *(ēpesen)* him greatly." Therefore he married her in all splendor.[89]

It is thus probable that the motif of the "little girl" who "pleases" King Herod Antipas in Mark 6:22 also derives from the Esther 1-2 complex.

H. The Offer of Half the Kingdom, a Vow, Fear, and Haste

The result of the "little girl" Salome's "pleasing" Herod Antipas so much by dancing at his birthday banquet is that the "king" says to her: "Ask me for whatever you wish, and I will give it to you." He then underscores this offer by vowing: "Whatever you ask me, I will give you, even half of my kingdom" (Mark 6:22-23). Salome's request is then hastily carried out.

I suggest that these three motifs also derive from Judaic haggada on the Scroll of Esther: the offer of half the kingdom, a vow to underscore this, and the haste of the offer's implementation. In addition, the motif of Herod Antipas' "fear" of the Baptist (Mark 6:20) stems from the same traditions.

1) Half the Kingdom

The term "asking" *(aiteō)* extends over the four verses of Mark 6:22-25. It thus dominates the plot, moving it onwards, at this central point of the Baptist narrative. In v. 23 the offer of the "king" is then expanded to include up to half his kingdom.

The latter phrase is not simply a "proverbial reference for generosity," as W. Lane labels it.[90] Nor are Luke 19:8 and 1 Kgs. 13:8, often mentioned by the commentators, at all relevant here. They lack half the "kingdom." It has also been observed, as by H. Anderson, that "as a puppet of Rome, Herod had not the ghost of a chance of giving *half* of his *kingdom* away."[91]

The latter phrase has nothing to do with historical reality. It also derives from the Esther narrative. Although this has often been asserted, I would now

---

[89]Clines 222-23. The second statement also appears to be based on v. 17 of the Hebrew text. The Persian's great sex drive is also emphasized in the midrashim and targums. Cf., for example, 1 Targ. Est 2:2 (Grossfeld 45 and n. 6 on p. 90) and 2:14 (Grossfeld 47 and n. 29 on p. 101).

[90]See his *The Gospel According to Mark* (NICNT, 2; Grand Rapids, Michigan: Eerdmans, 1974) 221, after referring to Est 5:3, 6.

[91]See his *The Gospel of Mark* (NCB, 2; London: Oliphants, 1976) 169. The offer of Gaius Caligula to Herod Agrippa II at a banquet in *Ant.* 18.289-304 also has nothing to do with "half a kingdom." It is noted by Pesch, *Das Markusevangelium* 342, n. 22.

like to suggest why the author of the Baptist narrative again borrowed from the Scroll of Esther here.

In the MT of Est 5:3 King Ahasuerus says: "What is it, Queen Esther? What do you ask for?[92] Up to half the kingdom, and it will be given you!" This is repeated with slight variations in 5:6 and 7:2. The first part of the offer is also found in 9:12.

Just as in Mark 6:22-23, King Ahasuerus' offer is expressed in a triad: What is it? What do you ask for? Up to half the kingdom will be given you. In contrast to the tetrarch Herod Antipas, the Persian king could indeed have given Esther half his realm. In Est 1:1 it is described as reaching from India to Ethiopia, and as comprising 127 provinces. In rabbinic tradition on this verse, the king first loses all his kingdom, then regains half of it at his marriage to Esther, and the second half at the death of Haman.[93]

The LXX of Est 5:3 employs *ti theleis;* ("What do you want?"), the same Greek term as found in Mark 6:22 and 25. It also adds the possessive pronoun "my" to "kingdom." The Greek verb employed in Mark, *aiteō,* is only found in the similar passage LXX "A" of Est 5:6.[94] Both in LXX and "A" of 7:2 the related noun *aitēma* is employed.[95]

The first targum to Est 5:3, however, shows most similarity to the Marcan narrative. It reads:

> The king then said to Esther: What do you need, Queen Esther? And what is your request? Even if you were to ask for half of my kingdom, I would give it to you – except (the request for the re-) building of the Holy Temple, which stands within the border of half of my kingdom, I cannot grant you. For thus I have promised with an oath to Geshem the Arab, to Sanballat the Horonite, and Tobiah the Ammonite slave, that I would not permit it to be rebuilt. For I am afraid of the Jews lest they rebel against me. This request I cannot grant you. But whatever else you shall ask of me, I shall decree that it should be promptly done, and that your wish shall be granted to you.[96]

As Grossfeld points out, the targum here changes the Hebrew passive verb "and it will be given (to you)" to the active: "I (the king) will give it."[97] This

---

[92]See BDB 134-35 on בקשׁ: seek, desire, ask, request.

[93]See Midr. Ps. 22/26 on Ps 22:17 (Braude 1.320), a comment by the early Tanna R. Nehemiah; 1 Targ. Est 1:1 (Grossfeld 5 and 40; see also his n. 9 on p. 78); and the other sources noted in Ginzberg, *The Legends* 6.457, n. 47.

[94]Clines 234-35, in his numeration 6:17.

[95]For the "A" test, see Clines 238-39, in his numeration 8:1.

[96]Grossfeld 59, whose punctuation I have slightly changed for easier reading. The Aramaic is found on pp. 22-23. Grossfeld cites rabbinic parallels to the Temple haggada on p. 147, n. 16 (the page number in Buber's edition of Aggadat Esther is, however, not 51, but 53).

[97]Grossfeld 146, n. 15. For another grammatical change, see his n. 14.

corresponds exactly to the active form found in Mark 6:22-23: "I (King Herod Antipas) will give it." In addition, the first targum has "my" kingdom, as in Mark 6:3. I therefore suggest that the tradition still found in the first targum to Est 5:3 provided the narrator of the Baptist account with his imagery of a king's offering a "girl" up to "one half of his kingdom."

In addition to "half of my kingdom," three other aspects still found in the first targum on Est 5:3 influenced the Baptist narrative: an oath, fear, and haste.

2) An Oath

Except for Peter's swearing in 14:71, the only occurrence of *omnyō* in Mark is in the Baptist narrative at 6:23. After offering her whatever she wants, "King" Herod Antipas here "swears/vows" to Salome to give her up to half his kingdom. This is reflected in v. 26, which speaks of the king's "oaths" *(horkos)*, plural, a term found only here in Mark.

I suggest that this rare Marcan motif of swearing by an oath is also derived from Judaic haggada on Esther. The first targum to Est 5:3 quoted above, for example, describes the king's willingness to give Esther whatever she wants, even up to half the kingdom. The one exception, however, is the (re-)building of the Jerusalem Temple, for the king promised "with an oath" (בִּשְׁבוּעָה) not to permit this.[98] This is also found in the same targum to 5:6 and 7:2.[99] In addition, the motif is found in the LXX "A" text on Est 7:5: "But the king *swore (omnyō)* that she (Esther) should tell him who had behaved so arrogantly as to do this, and with an *oath (horkos)* he undertook to do for her whatever she wished."[100] The latter phrase is very close to Mark 6:23.

3) Fear

Although his new wife Herodias had a grudge against John the Baptist and wanted to kill him, Mark 6:20 strangely relates that she was at first unable to do so. The reason was that Herod "feared" *(phobeomai)* John, knowing him to be a righteous and holy man. He therefore "preserved" him.

Herod Antipas' "fear" of John lacks any kind of motivation here. Josephus, however, relates that the real reason for the tetrarch's putting John in chains and having him put to death in the wilderness fortress of Machaerus was his "fearing" *(deidō)*[101] sedition, an uprising, an upheaval, due to John's

---

[98]Aramaic in Grossfeld 23.
[99]*Ibid.*, 23 and 28, respectively.
[100]See Clines 238-39, in his numeration 8:7.
[101]LSJ 373: *"fear,* dist. from *phobeomai";* be alarmed, anxious; fear, dread.

popularity.[102]   The Greek term for "sedition" here is *stasis*,[103] for which the MS variant reads *apostasis:* "defection, revolt."[104]

The same knowledge of Herod Antipas' "fearing" John the Baptist because of a possible revolt, which was available to Josephus at the end of the first century C.E., may also have been available to the author of the Baptist narrative. Yet it could instead derive from a tradition still found in the first targum to Est 5:3. There Ahasuerus states: "I am *afraid* of the Jews lest they rebel against me." The Aramaic term here, דְּחֵיל, means: "to fear, be afraid of." But it can also mean "to worship, revere."[105] Herod Antipas' "fearing" John the Baptist may involve the connotation of "revering" him: he was a righteous and holy man (Mark 6:20). This strange use of "fearing" thus may derive from the Aramaic term also employed in the targum. It would also have been easy for the narrator to understand the plural "Jews" (יְהוּדָאֵי) as the singular "Jew" (יְהוּדָאֵי); the consonants remain the same.[106] King Ahasuerus feared Jews or a Jew; "King" Herod Antipas feared/respected the Jew John.[107] The political theme of rebellion found in the targum and in Josephus is left out in Mark, and the moral accusation of marrying a living brother's former wife is emphasized instead.[108]

4) Haste

It is striking how often the motif of "haste" occurs in the Marcan narrative after Salome is given one free wish from the "king." In 6:25-27 she enters the banquet room "immediately with haste" *(euthys meta spoudēs)* and asks that John's head be given her "at once" *(exautēs)*. The king therefore "immediately" *(euthys)* sends a bodyguard/executioner to bring it.

This great emphasis on "haste" is not simply due to the narrator's desire for swift action at this point. While there is a tendency in Judaic haggadic accounts

---

[102]*Ant.* 18.118 in the English translation of L. Feldman.

[103]LSJ 1634: faction, sedition, discord.

[104]*Ibid.*, 218.

[105]Jastrow 23.

[106]*Ibid.*, 566.

[107]It should be noted that the evangelist Matthew, aware of Mark 11:32 (the Jerusalem authorities "were afraid of the people, for all held that John was a real prophet"), changed Mark 6:20 from Herod's fearing John to his "fearing the people, because they held him (John) to be a prophet."

[108]If John employed language of rebuke for Herod Antipas similar to that which he used for people even willing to be baptized by him ("You brood of vipers!" in Matt 3:7 and Luke 3:7), it is understandable that the tetrarch became greatly annoyed at him. Josephus hints at agreement with John's position in *Ant.* 18.136, where Herodias is said to have "flouted the ways of our fathers" by marrying Herod Antipas, the living brother of her former husband (see n. 162 below).

to add such a specific detail,[109] I suggest that the motif of "haste" in the Marcan Baptist narrative also derives from the tradition still found in the first targum on Est 5:3, as well as from 5:5.

The first targum at 5:3 has King Ahasuerus tell Esther: "Whatever else you shall ask of me, I shall decree that it should be *promptly* done, and that your wish shall be granted to you." The Aramaic term here for Grossfeld's translation "promptly" is literally "with haste": בִּבְהִילוּ.[110]

Secondly, in the MT of Est 5:5 the king tells his servants: "*Bring* Haman *quickly* so that (we) may do Esther's matter." The first targum renders the מַהֲרוּ of the MT by אוֹחִיוּ: "*Bring* Haman *immediately,* in order to carry out the ordered decree of Esther...."[111] This emphasis in 5:5 on the haste with which Esther's wish is to be implemented is embedded between vv. 3 and 6, in which the king's promise of up to half his kingdom is expressed. I therefore suggest that the motif of haste still found in the first targum on Est 5:3, as well as in v. 5, provided the background for the great emphasis on the haste with which Salome's request is carried out in the Marcan Baptist narrative.[112]

I. The King's Order to Have a Bodyguard/Executioner Behead John; the Baptist's Head on a Platter.

After consulting with her mother Herodias, Salome asks "King" Herod Antipas to give her at once the head of John the Baptist on a platter. Adhering to his vow(s), the king sends off a bodyguard, ordering him to bring John's head. The soldier departs, decapitates John in prison, brings his head upon a platter, and gives it to the "little girl," who in turn gives it to her mother (Mark 6:24-28).

Nowhere else in the NT, the LXX, Philo, or Josephus does the word for "bodyguard" in v. 27 *(spekoulatōr)* occur. Also, except for Matthew's retelling of the Baptist narrative, the term "platter" *(pinax)* in 6:25 and 28 is found only one more time in the NT.[113] The rareness of these two terms, plus the improbably gruesome character of the episode, justify searching for their origin elsewhere.

---

[109]Cf., for example, *Ant.* 11.267, where Josephus has Ahasuerus order Haman to be hanged "at once," which is lacking in the MT of Est 7:10.

[110]Jastrow 142. The verb בָּהַל means to hurry, and the noun בֶּהָלָה, "suddenness" *(ibid.).*

[111]Grossfeld 23 and 59. On the verb יְחִי, see Jastrow 574. The second targum employs here סַרְהֵב (Cassel Aramaic 58; see Jastrow 1023).

[112]Cf. also the motif of haste in Est 2:9; 3:15; 6:10, 12, 14 (bring Haman "in haste" to the banquet); and 8:14. See also section 1) below on the haste of a bodyguard's decapitating a victim.

[113]See Luke 11:39, where Jesus says the Pharisees cleanse the outside of the cup and the "dish" (RSV).

1. A Bodyguard

Herod the Great, the father of Herod Antipas, once received from Caesar 400 Gauls as a bodyguard (doryphoros, literally "spear-bearer").[114] In addition, there were Thracians and Germans in the greater contingent.[115] The names of several, designated sōmatophylax, are even known.[116] One instance relates that the Idumean king "instantly" sent his bodyguards to kill his own son, Antipater.[117] Philo relates Herod Agrippa I, the brother of Herodias, had a "bodyguard of spearmen, decked in armour overlaid with gold and silver."[118] Finally, Bernice, the wife of Herod Agrippa II mentioned in Acts 25:13, 23 and 26:30, also had her own bodyguards.[119] The mention of a bodyguard of Herod Antipas in Mark 6:27 thus fits into the Herodian family picture, although he was only a tetrarch.

The Greek term spekoulatōr is actually a Latin loan word, speculator. One meaning of the term is an army scout or spy. Yet the meaning in Mark 6:27 is a soldier assigned to a leader's headquarters to guard him. That is, he is a "bodyguard." One of his official tasks was the execution of condemned persons.[120] The latter is stated well by Josephus in Ant. 19.42: "a post as his bodyguards (doryphoros) and public executioners."[121]

The word spekoulatōr also entered rabbinic Hebrew and Aramaic.[122] Num. Rab. Balak 20/14 on Num 22:23 states, for example: "When a mortal king sends an executioner to kill a man...."[123] 'Abot R. Nathan A 38 also relates that both Rabban Simeon b. Gamaliel and R. Ishmael b. Elisha asked the spekoulatōr for the privilege to be killed first. When the lot fell to Simeon to die first, "immediately (מִיָּד) he took his sword and cut off his head."[124]

---

[114]Josephus, Ant. 15.217 and Bell. 1.397.

[115]Bell. 1.672; Ant. 17.198.

[116]Bell. 1.576; Ant. 16.314; 17.55.

[117]Bell. 1.664; Ant. 17.187 ("without delay and on the instant").

[118]Flacc. 30 in the translation of F. Colson.

[119]Bell. 2.310.

[120]See the sources listed in the article "Speculatores" by F. Lammert in Pauly-Wissowa's Realencyclopädie, Zweite Reihe, sechster Halbband 1583-86, especially 2.a). The term should not be confused with spiculator, for which Lammert also wrote the article, 1760-62.

[121]For a number of Roman references to the speculator, see also J. Wettstein, Novum Testamentum Graecum, Tomus I (Amsterdam, 1752; reprint Graz, 1962) 580-81.

[122]See Krauss, Lehnwörter 2.409.

[123]Soncino 6.800.

[124]Hebrew in S. Schechter, Aboth de Rabbi Nathan (New York: Feldheim, 1945; reprint of Vienna, 1887) 114. The English is found in J. Goldin, The Fathers According to Rabbi Nathan (New Haven: Yale University, 1955) 160. See also Lev. Rab. Emor 26/2 on Lev 21:1 (Soncino 4.327) for the designation by R. Simeon b. Yochai, a third-generation Tanna (Strack and Stemberger, Einleitung 82-83), of the serpent (Satan) as "the executioner." That is, Satan causes death.

The passage with *spekoulatōr* which is decisive for the Marcan narrative, however, derives from Judaic haggada on the Scroll of Esther. Before evaluating it, several observations on King Ahasuerus' "bodyguards" are helpful.

In Est 2:21 two of the king's eunuchs, Bigthan and Teresh, "guard" the threshold of the palace. The LXX already calls them here *archisōmatophylakes*, "chiefs of the bodyguard." In Est. Rab. 6/13 on this verse they are designated קלסריקין.[125] This term does not mean "Coele-Syrians," or "fools," as suggested by Jastrow.[126] Rather, as proposed by Levy, it represents a corruption of the Greek *kolastēr*, "executioner,"[127] designating a major task of the bodyguards.

In Panim Achérim 2 on Est 6:1 Mordecai sees Haman coming, "and the סְפָּקְלְטוֹר with him."[128] Here the bodyguard of the king is called by the same term as in Mark 6:27.

The major influence on Mark 6:27, however, derives from Judaic haggada on Est 5:2, directly adjacent to the very important verse three analyzed above. At the end of the first century C.E., in his comment on Est 2:21, Josephus inserts in *Ant.* 11.205 something on Est 5:2.[129] He notes that around Ahasuerus' "throne there stood men with *pelekeis* to punish any who approached the throne without being summoned."[130] The Greek word employed here means a two-edged axe, a battle axe, an "executioner's axe."[131] That is, Josephus was also aware of Ahasuerus' bodyguards' function of executing the condemned. This is corroborated by the following similar tradition.

The second targum on Est 5:2 relates that "when the king saw Queen Esther standing in the court, she found favor and grace in his sight. But the royal *executioners* (אִסְפָּקְלְטוֹרֵי) who stood there were ready to kill, to kill Esther."[132] The latter two verbs are different in Aramaic, the second being קְטַל. Its first meaning is "to cut," and secondly "to kill."[133] The connotation is that the executioners are ready, if the king so wishes, to kill Esther by "cutting" (off her head). Similar terminology is found in 1 Targ. Est 1:19, which states that if Vashti "come before the king, let the king decree (literally 'cut'),[134] and he (the executioner) will remove her head. Then let the king give her royal position to

---

[125]Lewin-Epstein 18b.

[126]Jastrow 1380 and 1373.

[127]See Levy 4.315, who cites the Yalqut on this verse as well as other examples of the king's "executioner," and LSJ 971.

[128]Hebrew in Buber, *Aggadic Books* 75, bottom.

[129]See also *Ant.* 11.238-39 for this haggadic motif in the context of Est 5:2.

[130]English by R. Marcus in the LCL.

[131]LSJ 1357.

[132]Aramaic in Cassel 57-58; English in Cassel 325.

[133]Jastrow 1349. It is also employed in 1 Targ. Est 1:1 of Vashti's being "killed" naked. See Grossfeld 5.

[134]Jastrow 231 on גזר.

another who is better than she."[135] Vashti is thus in danger here of having the executioner bodyguards of the king remove her head. It is precisely this motif of "cutting off one's head," tied to this same verse in Esther (1:19), which also provides the background imagery for the Baptist's head on a platter.

2. The Baptist's Head on a Platter

Judaic interpreters of Esther were struck by the fact that the manner of Vashti's death is totally lacking in the Hebrew text at Est 1:19. It simply states that "Vashti is to come no more before King Ahasuerus." Since she is not described as being banned to a remote province,[136] and because the king soon remarries, curiosity bred the invention of explanations as to how Vashti met her end.

The LXX of Est 2:1 already notes that the king had "condemned" (katakrinō) Vashti (to death). His having her "executed" is related in a large number of rabbinic sources.[137] The Hebrew verb employed is הָרַג, "to kill," which in legal contexts means decapitation by the sword, as in m. Sanh. 7:3.[138] The most important rabbinic passages for the Marcan narrative are Est. Rab. 4/9 on Est 1:19, and 4/11 on Est 1:21.[139] The first relates the offer of Memucan before the king in regard to Est. 1:19, "If it please the king, let there go forth a royal

---

[135]Aramaic in Grossfeld 9. I have slightly modified his English on p. 44: "that her head be cut off." The second targum on Est 7:9 (Cassel Aramaic 66, English 335) adds the detail that the sword of the king was employed to behead the nobles of the kingdom, certainly including Vashti.

[136]This may, however, be the connotation of ekballō in Ant. 11.195. See LSJ 501, I.2. The meaning "to divorce" (I.4) is improbable.

[137]Many are listed in The Legends 6.456, n. 42. Add to these Midr. Ps. 22/24 on Ps 22:12 (Buber 193; Braude 1.319), and 22/26 on Ps 22:17 (Buber 194; Braude 1.320). The latter passage is a statement by the early Tanna R. Nehemiah. See also the first targum to Esther on 2:1 and 5:1 (Grossfeld 44 and 58), and the second targum on Est 1:12 and 16 (Cassel English 295 and 296). In b. Meg. 12b the reading of the Munich MS is: "Therefore it was decreed that she should be killed naked on Sabbath" (Soncino 71, n. 2).

[138]Danby's translation in The Mishnah 391 is: "The ordinance of them that are to be beheaded [is this]: they used to cut off his head with a sword as the government does. R. Judah says: This is shameful for him; but, rather, they lay his head on a block and cut if off with an axe. They said to him: There is no death more shameful than this." Billerbeck called attention to this passage in Str-B 1.683 and 270; see also Grossfeld 181, n. 10. The second targum on Est 1:16 (Cassel Aramaic 34, English 296-97) has Memucan, the youngest minister, give his advice regarding execution first. This reflects Jewish legal procedure in a capital case, as prescribed by m. Sanh. 4:2 (Danby 387). On this, see y. Sanh. 4:8(2), 22b, where Est 1:16 is cited (English in J. Neusner, The Talmud of the Land of Israel, 31: Sanhedrin and Makkot [Chicago: University of Chicago, 1984] 142), and Est. Rab. 4/6 on Est 1:16 (Soncino 9.60-61).

[139]Their relevance was already pointed out by Wettstein in 1752. See his Novum Testamentum Graecum, Tomus I, p. 413 on Matt 14:11.

order": "He said to him (the king), 'My lord the king, say but a word and I will bring in her head on a platter.'"

It is important to recall here that the first targum on Est 1:19, cited above in 1), also says that if the king so decrees (literally "cuts"), he (Memucan or the executioner) will remove Vashti's head.

The second passage in Esther Rabbah comments on Est 1:21, "This advice pleased the king and the princes, and the king did as Memucan proposed": "He gave the order. And he brought in her head on a platter."[140]

The hiphil of the term כָּנַס is employed in both Esther Rabbah comments. It means "to bring in."[141] That is, as in Mark 6:27-28, the room from which the victim's head is to be brought is considered nearby.

The phrase I have translated as "He gave the order" is the Hebrew גָּזַר, "to cut, decree" (see above). A wordplay may also be intended here: The king "cut," and Vashti's head was "cut off."

It should also be noted that only one person performs the decapitation in the Esther Rabbah accounts. This is also true of the bodyguard/executioner (spekoulatōr) in Mark 6:27-28.

Finally, the term translated "platter" in the Vashti account above is the Greek loan word in Hebrew, דִּיסְקוֹס: diskos. As here, it can mean a serving dish or trencher.[142] It should be noted that the Old Latin translates the term for "platter" in Mark 6:25 and 28, pinax,[143] with the same word: discus.[144] Diskos and pinax are thus synonyms, both meaning a serving dish, platter, or plate. The term דִּיסְקוֹס in Esther Rabbah on 1:19 and 21 is appropriate for the executioner's use because Judaic tradition says there were such platters at Ahasuerus' banquet. Midrash Panim Achérim 2 on Est 1:7 states in regard to the phrase "vessels differing from vessels": "And there were cups and platters (דּוֹסְקוֹת) there, of various kinds."[145] The bodyguard/executioner of Herod

---

[140]Hebrew in Lewin-Epstein 15a. An English translation is found in Soncino 9.61-62. See also Str-B 1.683.

[141]Jastrow 650.

[142]LSJ 437. See also the examples cited by Jastrow 302, and Krauss, Lehnwörter 2.209, 2). See especially b. Shab. 119a (Soncino 586), where R. Chiyya b. Abba, a fifth-generation Tanna (Strack and Stemberger, Einleitung 87-88), relates an incident in which a golden banquet table is brought into the room by sixteen men; there are "plates," goblets, pitchers, and flasks on it.

[143]Cf. LSJ 1405, "2. trencher, platter." See also J. Moulton and G. Milligan, The Vocabulary of the Greek New Testament Illustrated from the Papyri and Other Non-Literary Sources (Grand Rapids, Michigan: Eerdmans, 1957) 513.

[144]See A. Jülicher, W. Matzkow and K. Aland, eds., Itala. Das Neue Testament in altlateinischer Übersetzung. II Marcus-Evangelium (Berlin: de Gruyter, 1970²) 52. It also employs the term speculator in 6.27.

[145]Buber, Aggadic Books 59. This is also found in Yalqut Shim'oni § 1048 on Est 1:7, with the spelling דסקיות. See also the correct assumption by A. Loisy,

Antipas is also pictured as taking such a "platter" from the banquet table and putting the Baptist's head on it.

J. The King's Great Grief at an Innocent Victim

When "King" Herod Antipas heard Salome's request for the head of John the Baptist on a platter, according to Mark 6:26 he became "exceedingly sorry" about it. This is because Herod knew the prophet was a "righteous and holy man," whom he gladly heard (vv. 20-21). I suggest that both these motifs, the king's remorse and an innocent victim, also derive from haggadic development of the Scroll of Esther.

1. Great Grief

Herod Antipas' "becoming exceedingly sorrowful" in Mark 6:26 is *perilypos genomenos* in Greek. Its only other occurrence in Mark is in the Gethsemane scene, where Jesus says in 14:34: "My soul is very sorrowful, even to death."[146] In the Baptist narrative, the king's great remorse derives from a) King Ahasuerus' grief at Vashti's refusal to appear before him, and b) his remorse at executing his queen, who really was undeserving of this punishment.

a) Est 1:12 relates that when Queen Vashti refused to appear before him, the king was "very angry" (מְאֹד ... וַיִּקְצֹף); his anger even "burned within him." The LXX translates the first phrase with *elypēthē*. The verb *lypeō* in the active can also mean "to vex," but its primary meaning is "to grieve." The passive, however, as here, appears only to have the significance "to be grieved, distressed."[147] The LXX thus has Ahasuerus' anger preceded by grief. The "A" text follows this tendency, adding "greatly," as in the Hebrew: *elypēthē sphodra*.[148] Another way of expressing this in Greek would be by the adjective in Mark 6:26, *perilypos:* greatly grieved, very sorrowful. Although I am aware of no other interpretation of Est 1:12 as including the king's grieving before deciding to put away his queen, the LXX shows that this tradition is very old. It is also mirrored in Judaic comment on 2:1.

L'Évangile selon Marc (Paris: Nourry, 1912) 185: "On a platter, without doubt one of the platters which were circulated at the royal table." It should be noted that both the "transformation" motif in essay "One" and the "various" vessels here, including "platters," stem from haggadic interpretation of Est 1:7.

[146]This is taken over in Matt 26:38. The only other NT usage of the term is Luke 18:23.

[147]LSJ 1065. The Hebrew קָצַף never means "to grieve." See BDB 893 and Jastrow 1406: "to be angry." Other passages in the LXX where קָצַף is rendered by *lypeō* are 1 Kgs. 29:4; 4 Kgs. 13:19; Est 2:21; Isa 8:21 and 57:17. See also LXX Dan 2:12, where *perilypos* translates the Aramaic "very angry."

[148]Clines 220-21. His English translation of "vexed" should be changed to "grieved."

b) Some haggadic traditions maintain that Vashti stripped Jewish girls naked and made them work on the Sabbath. Because of "what she had done" (Est 2:1), the king required her to appear naked before him and his fellow banqueters on the seventh day (1:10), the Sabbath. When she refused, he in his drunken stupor had her executed.[149] Another tradition on Est 2:1 states that she was executed because she would not allow the king to permit the rebuilding of the Jerusalem Temple.[150]

Other traditions, however, maintain that Vashti's punishment was undeserved. When the king ordered her to appear naked, she sent him word that her noble birth prevented such a display, which also might endanger his own further reign as king.[151]

Josephus says that Vashti, observing the laws of the Persians, who do not allow their wives to be seen by strangers, refused to appear before the king and his fellow banqueters.[152] The "severe punishment" for her refusal to comply was his sending her away.[153]

Because of the law found in Est 1:20-22, the Jewish historian also notes that King Ahasuerus could not be reconciled to Vashti, although he loved her and suffered under their separation. Thus he "continued to grieve" in regard to what he desired, but which was no longer possible for him.[154] The Greek for "to grieve" here is the participle of *lypeō,* the same root as in the term "exceedingly sorrowful" in Mark 6:26. In this comment on Est 2:1, Josephus' special mention of the grief's "continuing" emphasizes its duration and suggests its intensity.

This first-century emphasis on the king's grief is reflected in Est. Rab. 5/2, also on Est 2:1. It relates: "After he had killed her he began to feel remorse, because he realized that she had acted properly."[155] The phrase for "feeling remorse" here is תְּהִי בֵּיהּ חֹוֶר.[156] The verb חָזַר with בְּ means to retract or repent.[157] That is, King Ahasuerus now deeply regretted his decision, made while drunk with wine. He felt grief over it, just as King Herod Antipas became "extremely sorrowful" at the execution of John the Baptist.

---

[149]See b. Meg. 12b, with the reading of the Munich MS (Soncino 71), as well as other sources cited in Ginzberg, *Legends* 6.455, n. 34.

[150]Est. Rab. 5/2 on Est 2:1 (Soncino 9.69). See also other sources cited in *Legends* 6.457, n. 48.

[151]See Est. Rab. 3/14 on Est 1:12 (Soncino 9.54) as well as other sources cited in *Legends* 6.456, n. 36.

[152]*Ant.* 11.191.

[153]*Ant.* 11.194.

[154]*Ant.* 11.195.

[155]Soncino 9.69.

[156]Lewin-Epstein 16b.

[157]Jastrow 446.

I suggest that the great grief of King Ahasuerus found in Judaic interpretation of Est 1:12 and 2:1 provided the motif of King Herod Antipas' great grief in Mark 6:26.

2. An Innocent Victim

According to the midrash on Est 2:1 just cited, the Persian king realized that Vashti had acted "properly." The Hebrew term for this is כְּהוֹגֶן, which means appropriately, rightly, properly.[158] This is emphasized by the next comment, dealing with "what was decreed against her": "contrary to what was right."[159] The Hebrew term for "right" here is the same one as before. The second targum on Est 2:1 also maintains Vashti's innocence, stating that "she herself did not deserve (שַׁוְיָא) punishment of death."[160] In Midrash Abba Gorion on Est 2:1 the king similarly tells those of his advisors who had suggested he have Vashti killed: "I did not act well." He then has the seven advisors killed for this.[161]

All of this stress on the innocence of Vashti, whose head was brought in to King Ahasuerus on a platter, provided part of the background for King Herod Antipas' view of John the Baptist as "righteous and holy" in Mark 6:20. Just as Vashti's refusal to appear naked before a banquet of drunken men did not deserve her execution, so John's rebuke of Herod Antipas for marrying his brother's wife while the latter was still alive, also did not deserve death.[162]

Finally, the same Palestinian tradition regarding John's positive character available to Josephus may also have been available to the author of the Baptist account. Josephus labels John a "good" *(agathos)* man, who had exhorted his fellow Jews to "virtue" *(aretē)*, "righteousness" *(dikaiosynē,* twice) toward one another, and "piety" *(eusebeia)* towards God.[163] The Jewish historian, originally from Jerusalem, thus speaks very positively about John, implying his innocence when Herod Antipas had him executed. If the Aramaic-speaking, Palestinian author of the Marcan Baptist account also knew of this popular description of John, he could easily have combined John's righteousness and piety with the tradition of Vashti's innocence to label him a "righteous and holy" man.

---

[158]Jastrow 336 on הוֹגֶן.

[159]Soncino 9.69.

[160]Aramaic in Cassel 35, English 298. See Jastrow 1533 on שַׁוְיָא: worthy of.

[161]The Hebrew is in Buber, *Aggadic Books* 17. Wünsche's German translation is found in *Aus Israels Lehrhallen* 2.107.

[162]For this prohibition, see Lev 18:16 and 20:21. The Levirate marriage obligation of Deut 25:5-10 thus did not apply here since the brother was still alive. For a German translation of Sifra on Lev 20:21, cf. Str-B 1.680. See also n. 108.

[163]*Ant.* 18.117.

VIII. THE ORIGINAL LANGUAGE, LITERARY FORM, CONTENT, AND ORIGIN OF THE BAPTIST NARRATIVE

The above ten similarities[164] between Judaic interpretation of the narrative of King Ahasuerus' banquet in Esther 1 and other sections of the Scroll, and the story of how the Baptist met his end in Mark 6:17-29, may be questioned individually. Cumulatively, however, they simply provide too many exact word and motif similarities for the latter to be dismissed as mere "reminiscences" of the former. Here I shall ask whether the materials analyzed in VII. can shed light on the original language, the literary form, the extent of the narrative of John's beheading, and its origin.

A. The Original Language

As indicated in the introduction, many commentators, following Wellhausen, have noted Aramaisms in the Marcan text. I also have suggested a Semitic wordplay found in the terms for "keep safe," "have a grudge against," and "prison." Since there is also no demonstrable direct influence of the LXX on the content of the narrative, and since many of the words (such as *spekoulatōr*) and motifs are found only in the Esther midrashim and targums, as well as in the account of Ahasuerus' feast in Josephus, whose native language was Aramaic, I find it most plausible to posit an original account in Aramaic, although Hebrew cannot be completely excluded.

When this narrative reached Jewish Christians, in bilingual environments, such as Syria, it was translated into Greek and took on specific terms such as "little girl," *korasion,* from the LXX version of Esther. The bilingual Jewish translator(s) recognized the dependency of the narrative on Judaic haggada on the Scroll of Esther and correctly borrowed terminology from the LXX version of that biblical book. The story then reached the author of the Gospel of Mark in Greek, most probably in written form.[165] Despite the relatively plain Koine Greek of the evangelist, he shows no signs of having Aramaic or Hebrew as his mother tongue.

---

[164]These become even more if the several motifs found in Section VII, H, for example, are included.

[165]See also the arguments of Lohmeyer, *Das Evangelium des Markus* 117.

B. The Literary Form

The Baptist narrative has been described as a "legend,"[166] a "popular folk-tale,"[167] a "Volkssage,"[168] a "midrash,"[169] or a haggadic *ma'ase*.[170] Legend, folk-tale and saga are very broad terms in English. In addition, they usually imply that the content of the narrative is either unhistorical or not to be taken seriously. The term "midrash," although employed more and more by NT scholars, really only applies to the verse by verse interpretation of a biblical book, for example Esther in b. Meg. 10b-17a.[171] A *ma'ase* in rabbinic sources is a specific example of a general statement, usually in a legal context.[172] Bowman, who applies the term here, assumes that Mark 6:16 is such a general statement.

Although I disagree with the latter, Bowman is nevertheless basically correct in his designation. Mark 6:16 states that Herod Antipas had "beheaded *(apokephalizō)* John. This verb is found in the NT only in the parallel tradition in Matt 14:10, and in Luke 9:9. Just as Judaic interpreters of Est 1:19 explained what happened to Queen Vashti by saying King Ahasuerus had her executed in a particular way, so the Jewish-Christian author of Mark 6:17-29 sought to explain exactly how John was "beheaded." To do so, he primarily relied on the most famous example of someone's being beheaded in Judaic tradition: Vashti, from the very popular Scroll of Esther.

I propose the term "etiological haggada" for the Baptist narrative. The story not only explains the cause of John's being beheaded (his rebuke of Herod Antipas for marrying his former sister-in-law while his own brother was still alive), but also fills in the manner of the beheading, something typical of haggada.[173]

---

[166]See R. Bultmann, *The History of the Synoptic Tradition* (New York: Harper & Row, 1963) 301; Klostermann, *Das Markus-evangelium* 58; as well as Grant, "The Gospel According to St. Mark" 734: "a popular legend."

[167]Anderson, *The Gospel of Mark* 167.

[168]Merx, *Das Evangelium Matthaeus* 228.

[169]See I. de la Potterie, "Mors Johannis Baptistae (Mc 6, 17-29)" in *VD* 44 (1966) 147.

[170]J. Bowman, *The Gospel of Mark*. The New Christian Jewish Passover Haggadah (Studia post-biblica 8; Leiden: Brill, 1965) 154.

[171]See Strack and Stemberger, *Einleitung* 223.

[172]*Ibid.*, 36. It is the thirteenth of the thirty-two middot. For such a *ma'ase*, see m. Yeb. 16:7 ("Once it happened that...") in Danby, *The Mishnah* 245.

[173]See I. Heinemann's term, "the creative writing of history," which fills in biblical narratives, quoted in Strack and Stemberger, *Einleitung* 225. Grossfeld in *The First Targum to Esther* iv defines haggada as "legendary recountings of incidents to supply gaps in the canonical history."

C. The Content

Almost all the commentators agree that the author of the Gospel of Mark found 6:17-29 in its present form, most probably already joined to vv. 14-16.[174] This makes much sense, for as I remarked above, the narrative is designed to explain why and how Herod Antipas had John "beheaded" in v. 16.

Only J. Gnilka proposes a slightly different original form of vv. 17-18: "Herod had married Herodias, the wife of his brother Philip. John said to him: 'It is not lawful for you to have the wife or your brother.' Herod then sent and seized John and bound him in prison." Because of Mark's connecting the whole narrative to vv. 14-16, Gnilka believes he was forced to transfer Herod's actions against John to the beginning.[175]

While this suggestion seems more logical to the modern reader in regard to sequence, the present form of vv. 17-18 is also quite understandable as they stand. The "beheading" of v. 16 may have recalled for the author of the narrative the place of that action, the prison of v. 17. He therefore set the scene there at the outset, and then he related how John got into prison.

Gnilka also suggests that "he heard him gladly" in v. 20 is a Marcan addition since the phrase is also found in 12:37, the only other occurrence of the term "gladly" in the gospels.[176] Yet the latter usage could just as well be borrowed from the former, leaving the first occurrence original.

Thirdly, Gnilka believes the term "the baptizer" in 6:24 is a redactional addition because it differs from "the Baptist" in v. 25.[177] It may, however, be due to the same form, "the baptizer," in v. 14 and seek to vary the style here by having a different Greek word form than that employed in v. 25. This would already have been done at a pre-Marcan stage of the Greek. Josephus also employs *baptistos* for John and two varying words for baptism in his short description of the prophet's activity: *baptismos* and *baptisis*.[178] No one considers one of the latter to be redactional. In both Mark and Josephus, the varying Greek forms probably seek to express adequately a Semitic original.[179]

Finally, I suggested in Section VII, D that the evangelist may have added the prefix *syn-* ("with") in Mark 6:22 to the basic form *hoi anakeimenoi,* "those

---

[174]See, for example, Pesch, *Das Markusevangelium* 337.

[175]*Das Evangelium nach Markus* (Mk 1 - 8, 26) 245.

[176]*Ibid.*

[177]*Ibid.*

[178]*Ant.* 18.116-17. See L. Feldman's n. "b" on p. 82 in the LCL edition.

[179]This is most probably טָבַל, meaning "to immerse" or "bathe for purification" in the qal, and "to immerse" someone or something in the hiphil. See Jastrow 517. Cf. also the variant forms הַטּוֹבֵל in Mark 6:14, and הַמַּטְבִּיל in vv. 24-25 in the Hebrew NT of Delitzsch (p. 72). The concept of a baptizer/baptist was new, thus the terminology was still fluent.

reclining (at table)," in v. 26 in order to vary the style. The Semitic form would have been the same in both cases.[180]

In summary, there are no convincing indications that the original content of the narrative of the death of John differed in any major way from what is still found in 6:17-29.

D. The Origin of the Narrative

A number of commentators believe the account of John's beheading arose in Baptist circles after the prophet's death.[181] This view is primarily based on Mark 6:29, the final note of the story: "When his disciples heard of it, they came and took his body, and laid it in a tomb."

It is true that there are no "Christian" features in this narrative, which is the only story in all the four gospels which is not centered on Jesus. Yet it was certainly not created by a non-Christian adherent of John, but by a follower of Jesus. As proposed above, it is dependent on the information given in Mark 6:14-16. That section explains how "King" Herod heard "it," the activities of Jesus (and his disciples). In contrast to others, who consider Jesus to be Elijah or a prophet as of old, Herod Antipas believes he is the resurrected John, whom he has beheaded.[182] The story, while dealing with the why and how of this "beheading," is thus part of the larger context concerned with who Jesus is not. By means of contrast, it helps to define the person of Jesus.

Gnilka, followed by Pesch, has maintained that the Baptist narrative was originally a martyr report comprised of vv. 17-18 and perhaps v. 29. This was then supplemented by a popular narrative.[183] As I have noted in the introduction, there is a Semitic wordplay in vv. 17, 19 and 20, making it improbable that vv. 19-29 were originally separate from vv. 17-18. While Judaic martyr reports certainly existed, the category "etiological haggada" employed above suffices. The primary interest of the original narrator was the why and how of John's death. The "why" implied martyrdom, yet the portrayal of John as a martyr was not the primary intention of the narrative.

---

[180]See Str-B 2.257, "2," for rabbinic examples of the Hebrew מְסוּבִּין for *anakeimenoi.*

[181]Cf. Anderson, *The Gospel of Mark* 167; J. Schniewind, *Das Evangelium nach Markus* (NTD 1; Göttingen: Vandenhoeck & Ruprecht, 1960) 61; J. Ernst, *Das Evangelium nach Markus* (RNT, 2; Regensburg: Pustet, 1981) 182; and H. Windisch, "Kleine Beiträge zur evangelischen Überlieferung" in *ZNW* 18 (1917) 73-81, p. 80.

[182]To this extent Herod's view in 6:16 agrees with the opinion of "some" in v. 14.   The Greek "they said" *(elegon),* the better reading here, is similar to the phrase in rabbinic Hebrew: יֵשׁ אוֹמְרִים, "some say." Or it literally translates אָמְרוּ, meaning "it is said, told...."   See Jastrow 598 and 79, respectively.

[183]See Gnilka's *Das Evangelium nach Markus* (Mk 1 - 8, 26) 246, and Pesch, *Das Markusevangelium* 1.338.

Other commentators posit a Hellenistic Jewish background for the author of the Baptist narrative. They primarily note affinities with the story of Xerxes (Ahasuerus) as related in Herodotus 9.108-13.[184] These have been analyzed elsewhere, and they need not be discussed here.[185] While the fifth-century B.C.E. Greek historian was certainly known to educated Hellenistic Jews, there is little possibility that a Hellenistic Jewish Christian borrowed *directly* from that narrative for his account of John's death. Rather, it is more probable that the Herodotus narrative was logically related by Hellenistic Jews at a very early time to the book of Esther, concerned with the same Persian king, Ahasuerus. Certain motifs from Herodotus entered the haggadic "filling in" of the Scroll, and thus the nonbiblical Hebrew and Aramaic Esther accounts.[186] It was from the latter, in turn, that the author of Mark 6:17-29 borrowed.

In conclusion, the original Aramaic language of the Baptist narrative, for which I have argued throughout, and the very close affinities with many terms and motifs found in the Hebrew Esther midrashim and in the targums, as well as in Josephus, whose mother tongue was Aramaic, all point to a Palestinian origin to the narrative. Syria, however, is also possible, where there were a number of bilingual communities.[187] This might account for the narrative's rapid translation into Greek before the author of Mark gathered the materials for his gospel, probably at the end of the sixties.[188]

IX.   THE NARRATIVE'S SIGNIFICANCE IN THE PRESENT CONTEXT

Mark 6:14-29 is not only inserted by the author of the gospel at this point to create the impression of a time lapse between Jesus' sending out the disciples in vv. 7-13, and their returning in v. 30. Other reasons are also involved.

---

[184]See Bultmann, *A History* 301; Klostermann, *Das Markusevangelium* 58; and W. Grundmann, *Das Evangelium nach Markus* (ThHNT 2; Berlin: Evangelische Verlagsanstalt, 1977[7]) 173. Gruesome decapitation episodes regarding Mark Anthony (Seneca, *Epistulas Morales* 83.25), a certain Flaminius (Livy 39.43), and Crassus (in Plutarch, *Crassus* 33), are interesting in regard to this particular motif, but show no other connection with the Baptist narrative.

[185]See Windisch, "Kleine Beiträge," himself dependent on A. Hausrath's *Neutestamentliche Zeitgeschichte* (Heidelberg: Bassermann, 1873[2]) 333.

[186]Examples could be the following: Xerxes, pleased with the daughter of his brother's wife, promises that she may have whatever she desires; he fears his wife's learning of this; on the king's birthday, at a royal feast, his vengeful wife, having waited until now, demands and receives her brother-in-law's wife, although the latter is innocent, and has her severely mutilated; the king very unwillingly consents to this; and the bodyguards of the king perform the cruel act.

[187]See also Lohmeyer, *Das Evangelium des Markus,* Ergänzungsheft 11.

[188]Cf. W. Kümmel, *Einleitung in das Neue Testament* (Heidelberg: Quelle & Meyer, 1983[21]) 70.

After the opening of the gospel, in which John baptizes Jesus in 1:9, Mark notes in v. 14 that only after the Baptist was "handed over" *(paradidōmi)*, that is, imprisoned, did Jesus enter Galilee and proclaim the gospel of God. Here distance is intentionally created between the two figures, who probably were of approximately the same age.[189] In 2:18-22 the fasting of John's disciples is mentioned, and the author stresses the newness of Jesus' message in regard to his predecessor. Mark 6:14-29, by means of a "flashback," completes the notice of John's imprisonment in 1:14 by stating the why and how of John's death in prison. Mark 8:28, a repetition of 6:14-16, also mentions the Baptist, as do 11:30 and 32.

All the references to John or his disciples after 1:14 thus point to the prophet as belonging to the past, the old age. By means of contrast, Jesus is portrayed as belonging to the present, the completely new age. In his life and ministry something qualitatively new has begun.

Secondly, and here at least the direction of Gnilka's "martyr report" is in part valid, the Baptist's imprisonment and death point ahead to Jesus' being taken prisoner, his suffering, and death. The Greek used of John in 1:14, "to be handed over," is the same term as employed of Jesus' Jerusalem passion in 9:31, 10:33, and numerous other places.[190] That is, for the Gospel of Mark John the Baptist not only provides a contrast to Jesus, he also is the primary model on which Jesus' betrayal and death are based. As John preached a baptism of repentance (1:4), and was imprisoned ("handed over") and executed, so Jesus preached repentance (1:15), was handed over, made a prisoner (15:1), and executed.

Finally, A. Loisy astutely notes that John the Baptist in Mark 6:29 was buried in a tomb, from which he would never leave. This stands in distinct contrast to Jesus, who on Easter Sunday arose from his tomb (16:6),[191] and in the original, longer ending of Mark probably appeared to the disciples, showing victory over death and the grave.

X. WHAT THE NARRATIVE IS NOT

In conclusion, it is important to note what the Baptist narrative of Mark 6:17-29 does not say. By delimiting it, a justifiable interpretation of the text becomes more apparent. In addition to several other negative conclusions reached above, the following points are noteworthy. 1) The Baptist account is not about Herodias, as maintained by Lohmeyer,[192] or about Herod Antipas, as

---

[189]This is especially stressed by Luke in the first chapter of his gospel. Cf. 3:19; 14:10, 11, 18, 21, 41, 42, 44; and 15:1 (with binding), 10, 15.

[190]See also 8:31, the first passion prediction, directly after the mention of John the Baptist in v. 28, as well as 9:12-13.

[191]*L'Évangile selon Marc* 187.

[192]*Das Evangelium des Markus* 118.

M. Dibelius ascertained.[193] W. Schmithals provides a variant of the latter by implying that the narrative was related in order to substantiate the respect Herod showed John in 6:16.[194] Rather, it deals with the why and how of John's beheading. 2) The primary biblical background for the Baptist account is not that of Elijah and Jezebel (1 Kgs. 19:2), figures supposedly alluded to in John and Herodias.[195]   Nor is John a second Samuel.[196]   Rather, the Ahasuerus/Vashti narrative, as developed over the centuries in Judaic tradition on the Scroll of Esther, provides the major background. 3) The Marcan account is not an expansion of the Matthean version in 14:1-12, nor is the latter at least as old as the former, as maintained by A. Schlatter.[197] The Matthean version patently abbreviates Mark, making it later.[198] One example suffices to show this. The "bodyguard" of Mark 6:27 is omitted in Matt 14:10. If Mark were an expansion of Matthew, another common term such as *doryphoros* or *sōmatophylax* might be expected. Yet no Greek-speaking author would think of employing precisely at this point the rare term *spekoulatōr*, a Latin loan word. It is only because this term, which had entered Hebrew and Aramaic via the Greek, is found in Judaic haggadic traditions as a designation of King Ahasuerus' bodyguards, that it entered the Baptist narrative in Mark. The author of the Marcan account would not have added this rare term for bodyguard to Matthew. 4) The use of the Latin loan word *speculator* in Mark 6:27 has also been used by some scholars to help support the thesis that the gospel was written in Rome.[199] This is false, at least for this term. It instead derives from Palestinian Esther haggada. 5) Finally, the Baptist narrative is not historical, as claimed for example by H. Windisch[200] and W. Lane.[201] John instead met his end in chains in the wilderness fortress of Machaerus, as the Jewish historian Josephus relates (*Ant.* 18.119). There was no birthday banquet of a "King" Herod Antipas, no dancing of a "little girl" Salome before drunken men, no head dripping of blood brought in on a platter. Instead, the narrative from Judaic haggada on King Ahasuerus' birthday banquet, at which his innocent queen,

---

[193]See his *Die urchristliche Überlieferung von Johannes dem Täufer* (Göttingen: Vandenhoeck & Ruprecht, 1911) 80: "Its passive hero is the king"; "it is an anecdote about Herod."

[194]*Das Evangelium nach Markus. Kapitel 1-9, 1* (Ökumenischer Taschenbuchkommentar zum NT, 2/1; Gütersloh: Mohn; Würzburg: Echter, 1979) 313. See, however, also 315-16.

[195]See Loisy, *L'Évangile selon Marc* 181; Schniewind, *Das Evangelium nach Markus* 61; and many other commentators.

[196]Lohmeyer, *Das Evangelium des Markus* 119, coupled with Elijah.

[197]*Der Evangelist Matthäus* (Stuttgart: Calwer, 1929) 462.

[198]Cf. Kümmel, *Einleitung* 78.

[199]*Ibid.*, 69-70.

[200]"Kleine Beiträge" 78 and 80.

[201]*The Gospel According to Mark* 217. See also Pesch's remark in *Das Markusevangelium* 343 on Salome's dancing: "This unusual feature does not speak for its being invented."

Vashti, lost her head, provides the background for the questions of why and how Herod Antipas beheaded John. It does so in a typically Palestinian-Judaic way.[202] It fills in what is not explicitly stated in the text. The question of historicity should not be asked here. The narrative's "truth" in the setting of the gospel lies on a different level: John's death prefigures Jesus', and the Baptist's activity definitely ceases in the tomb. Through the resurrection from his own tomb, however, Jesus' activity continues or begins on a new level for those who confess him as the Son of God, the Lord of their lives.

---

[202]All six volumes of Ginzberg's *Legends* are full, for example, of such agadot. The tendency also continued in the apocryphal gospels of the early church.

Index of Modern Authors

Moore, C. 2, 4, 5, 7, 9, 25

Naveh, J. 6

Nilsson, M. 35, 36

Noetzel, H. 35, 37

Olmstead, A. 4-6

Paton, L. 2

Pesch, R. 49, 55, 68, 70

Potterie, I. de la 67

Sanders, J. N. 29

Schalit, A. 36

Schenk, W. 49

Schlatter, A. 16, 18, 72

Schmithals, W. 72

Schniewind, J. 69, 72

Schürer, E. 41, 42, 45, 48

Simon, M. 2, 4, 10

Smith, D. M. 30

Smitmans, A. 10

Stemberger, G. 2-4, 6, 8, 12, 13, 28, 43, 44, 52, 54, 60, 63, 67, 68

Strathmann, H. 30

Strauss, R. 39

Taylor, V. 49

Weege, F. 51

Weiss, B. 48

Wellhausen, J. 39, 49, 66

Wettstein, J. 60, 62

Wilde, O. 39

Windisch, H. 10, 69, 70

Wright, R. 28

ABOUT THE AUTHOR

Roger David Aus, b. 1940, studied at St. Olaf College, Harvard Divinity School, Luther Theological Seminary, and Yale University, from which he received the Ph.D. degree in 1971. He is an ordained clergyman of the Evangelical Lutheran Church in America, currently serving a German-speaking congregation in West Berlin, Germany. The Protestant Church of West Berlin kindly granted him a short study leave in Jerusalem, Israel, in 1981. His numerous articles on New Testament themes always reflect his great interest in, and appreciation of, the Jewish roots of the Christian faith.